# Your Money or Your Life: Time for Both

Martin Simon

Published by
Freedom Favours
The Exchange
Brick Row
STROUD
Gloucestershire
GL5 1DF
United Kingdom

November 2010



A CIP record for this book is available from the British Library.

ISBN 978-0-9566556-0-8

Book design and typography by Dave Thorp of The Workshop, marketing design consultancy.

Original Illustrations by Mariette Voke

Printed in Great Britain by Quorum Ltd.

Printed onto Cyclus Print 100% recycled paper stock manufactured from 100% post-consumer waste.

# Contents

# Foreword

## by Edgar Cahn

Your Money or Your Life: **Time for Both** reflects over ten years of dedicated and visionary work by Martin Simon forming the Timebanking movement in the United Kingdom and around the world. The book builds on his career as community organiser, change agent and public servant seeking to advance the public good. This book is an extraordinary gift because Martin always has one foot in the realm of specific deeds and acts – and another foot in the realm of ideas, of vision, of possibility. No matter where one opens this book, one finds Martin has captured the two types of energy that drive Timebanking.

The first kind of energy he celebrates is 'connectedness'. Much of the book emphasises ways in which Timebanking reduces the social isolation that one old-timer conveyed when he observed: *'We used to have community and then we got air conditioning!'*

Martin reveals how Timebanking undertakes to reclaim habitat for our species. And in doing so, he subtly reminds us that we cannot reclaim habitat for our species without reclaiming and sustaining habitat for all species. We are all linked. Our hunger for community celebrates that interdependence.

Lurking just below the surface of these examples is a second kind of energy that has driven Martin's life work and that drives Timebanking. He calls to us with a kind of urgency. He juxtaposes different sets of values to arouse us to disparities that he finds intolerable. His quotes, citations and illustrations are designed to ignite a kind of energy that my father called 'a sense of injustice'. We mobilize to redress unfairness when it offends our basic sense of decency. That lies behind Martin's stories of how Timebanking has been utilized by government, philanthropy, the independent sector and communities to remedy seemingly intractable social problems.

Martin provides chapter and verse demonstrating that every human being has something of value to contribute. He illustrates how Timebanking enlists every part of us, not just the part that goes on our résumés or CV. Page after page make a compelling case for valuing the ways that we can contribute that the market does not reward: caring labour, civic labour, cultural labour and environmental labour. Martin explains why Timebanking is uniquely able to do this: because it regards every hour as the most precious thing we can offer, our slice of eternity. By doing so, Martin makes clear that Timebanking does not just value what is scarce. It honours and values capacities that are abundant because they are universal.

Above all, this book conveys how and why Timebanking addresses a fundamental human need: the need to feel that we matter, that we can make a difference in the lives of others - and in doing so, that our acts can set in motion a process that can change the world. Martin Simon is both pioneer and prophet.

This meditation, 'Timebanking Math', tries to capture the spirit of this book:

**We take halting steps one by one by one**
**Our math is simple: one equals one equals one**
**One is tiny, the smallest absolute**
**But absolute is absolute**

**To be human is what we do and what we are**
**To care, to love, to reach out, to come to each other's rescue**
**To grieve, to celebrate, to reach consensus,**
**To stand up for what's right, to stand against what we know is wrong**

**These are not acquired though they may be honed**
**They are in our DNA - They are our being and our doing**
**Our shaping and creating and weaving**
**That's what one hour of our being means**

**We stand for what it means to be human**
**And human beings are not chattel;**
**There are domains which are above market, beyond price**
**Family, loved ones, justice, democracy, our planet,**
**all that is holy**
**Not for sale at market price, at any price**

**One hour, our piece of eternity.**
**Fleeting but nonetheless, precious, sacred, eternal**
**That is what Timebanking means, declares, affirms and reaffirms**
**We are - and We will not be diminished. Let it be.**

In Your Money or Your Life: Time for Both, Martin has laid down a choice and a challenge. We all are programmed to think we must wait for money. But Moses did not wait on a travel grant; Einstein did not wait on a research grant; Mandela did not wait on campaign financing.
So what are we waiting for?

That is what Martin Simon has asked all of us in this book.

**Dr Edgar S. Cahn**
*Creator of Time Dollars and founder of TimeBanks USA*
*See: wwwtimebank.org/founder.htm*

# Foreword by Jonathon Porritt

**If there was one word** that dominated the 2010 General Election it was 'change'. All three major parties just kept banging on and on about how they alone could transform our busted economic and social systems.

I only wish they actually meant it. I suspect we know, deep in our bones, that the next five years won't be very different from the last thirty years. Our dominant economic models will remain dominant. The pursuit of economic growth will remain the principal driver of public policy. We'll continue to bemoan worsening social ills, and to put a brave face on all those problems that we know could be sorted out if we really started to do things differently.

And that's what this little book will bring home to you in no uncertain terms. Martin Simon is not just an outstanding social entrepreneur, but a pioneering interpreter of new ways of thinking and acting. What he's done here is to bring together an up-to-the-moment account of the phenomenon of Timebanking (with one new Bank setting up every week here in the UK) with the latest thinking on delivering public services and rebuilding communities in radically different ways.

The essence of this convergence is a simple one. We really have two economies operating in the UK. The first is the monetised, growth-based, profit and tax generating economy that politicians spend 99.9% of their time obsessing about. The second is the core economy, largely unmonetised and based on stocks of social and human capital rather than financial capital. As Edgar Cahn, the founder of Timebanking, puts it: *'this economy constitutes the real work of society, which is caring, loving, being a citizen, a neighbour, and a human being.'*

This is supported by scientific evidence that human beings are 'hard-wired' to co-operate, and will enjoy more fulfilling and happy lives when they find a better balance between a life as a consumer and life as a caring neighbour or active citizen. We now have a social imperative to revalue people's time, everyday skills, caring and hospitality as natural resources to be used for our common good.

The two economies are not necessarily mutually exclusive, although the truth of it is that we're going to have to transform our growth-based economy in very short order if we're to avoid horrendous environmental and social breakdown. The two economies could even be mutually reinforcing – if only our political leaders recognised the true value of the core economy and created the kind of enabling framework which would permit it to prosper at a much greater scale – and with much greater recognition – than is currently the case.

In 2009, Baroness Julia Neuberger's Commission on the Future of Volunteering brought out an excellent report focusing in on the very powerful idea of *'putting mutuality back into the DNA of society'*.

It is of course perfectly possible to put a money value on volunteering (her Commission's Report estimated a net annual value at £36 billion and the Public Accounts Committee estimate that a further £23 billion is provided by informal carers), but in some respects that misses the point. Timebanking activists describe time committed to voluntary activities as 'social money' – money that is omnipresent, recession proof and limited only by the amount of time that any individual is able to commit. It offers people incentives and a safe framework to give and take, to exchange wisdom and skills, to lend their practical support and energy to strengthening the social environment. It cleverly uses new applications of IT to connect people once again to the places where they live. It is a genuinely sustainable, free local currency, utilising the human resources that are in plentiful supply, and that will actually grow the more they are carefully and responsibly nurtured.

So it doesn't necessarily make sense to try and 'bridge' these two economies via some kind of financial equivalence. But it does make sense to build that bridge around some of today's most important policy objectives: reinforcing social cohesion; improving the quality and cost-effectiveness of public services (particularly health, education and social services); empowering people to become more engaged citizens, and so on.

There's a whole new language around this in terms of 'co-production', 'personalisation', 'public goods', and so on. The language can sound clumsy, but the sentiments are spot on. Martin Simon argues that Timebanking is *'the ideal tool to deliver co-production in public services'* – with the government, professionals, relatives and volunteers all combining forces to deliver a totally different quality of public service. As Charlie Leadbeater says, *'relationships are at the core of effective public services'*.

And Timebanking is all about relationships. About the capacity for empathy. About nurturing and investing in our social environment. About a rediscovered compassion and everyday acts of kindness.

I guarantee that the personal stories and case studies will grab your attention. Timebanking is an inspired idea that is poised to inspire the lives of huge numbers of people as we set about the task of genuinely changing society.

# Introduction

**THE FIRST GLIMMER of an idea for this book came to me one hot, dusty evening in a large community hall near Galveston, Texas.**

I found myself there as part of a group of six social activists who had been invited over from the UK to train as community organisers. Barack Obama was being trained by the same organisation at around the same time, and he has often said that his real education did not take place at Harvard, but during his time working in Chicago as a community organiser. His election campaign used several community-organising techniques and it transformed communities as it moved across the USA and on into the White House. Thousands of new leaders and potential community organisers were recruited, many of whom were young people, and they confidently took charge of the first-ever Internet-based presidential campaign. They demonstrated that in these so-called apathetic and cynical times, all sorts of people will work together and co-operate en masse to bring about a future in which they all believe.

The training was tough going, but expertly led by Ed Chambers and Ernie Cortez, two larger-than-life characters, with a wealth of hard-won experience to share on building broad-based community organisations. We learned about how politicians and the 'powerful' operate, and I have used the valuable insights I gained ever since.

The training culminated in a practical piece of community organisation. Hundreds of families were assembled in the large community hall in rural

## Community organising

This is my potted version of how community organising works in practice:

1. Ask people how they think their lives could be improved and find out what each of them is prepared to do about it;

2. Think through with them the tactics necessary to achieve the changes that the majority (at least 80 percent) of them want to see; 'find the common ground and move forward together';

3. Take time to build caring and respectful relationships, discover people's interests and talents, use their connections and train up the natural leaders;

4. Find out who holds the power and meet with them face-to-face, preferably on your patch rather than on theirs;

5. Encourage local people to tell their stories and take action to influence those in power and to gain the support of the general public;

# in ten easy steps

6. Keep the pressure on and make it fun; whenever you can, use humour to draw attention to your issues and to expose the flaws in the opposing arguments;

7. Always be mindful of alternative, constructive ways forward, and be prepared to negotiate; remember that among politicians there are 'no permanent enemies and no permanent friends';

8. Remember that most people simply go along with the status quo and it only takes a well-organised 2% to 3% of the 'body politic' to initiate social change;

9. Make sure you maintain an equal balance between a hard head and a big heart;

10. The 'Iron rule' - never, never do for others what they can do for themselves.

Texas. They were ordinary law-abiding citizens, but determined to bring an end to years of under-investment in the infrastructure of their remote rural community. They were there to make things happen, to get the politicians and public services to act on their hitherto empty promises for an efficient, clean water supply and protection from soil erosion.

Senators, congressmen, mayors and a sheriff or two were escorted onto the stage by the local community organisers, with TV cameras and newspaper reporters positioned nearby. The evening was led meticulously by a team of local community organisers. Whenever local people spoke, their points were driven home by rapturous applause. When politicians prevaricated, they were met with silence; but, when they showed any sign of support for the local people's agenda, their words were received warmly. These responses had been rehearsed in small groups beforehand and, on the night, they were orchestrated by local leaders, each responsible for a block of around 50 people.

I was near the back of the hall and the block around me was being led by a large man in his late thirties, wearing jeans and a sweatshirt – not at all your typical college-educated activist. I noticed that his three young children, aged from about six to 13 years, were sitting by him, and I will never forget the way that those children watched their father's every move. They were so proud of him and of what he was doing to help their family and their local community. From time to time he would turn towards his children and they would all exchange the most enormous smiles. I was deeply moved. Dad was 'doing good' and his children loved him for it.

I thought about all the stories the family would have to tell about how they had brought clean water to their homes (by the end of the night the families were given firm assurances it would happen – on camera!). I imagined how this mutual respect would manifest itself time and again in their lives, as a family and with their neighbours as a community. I came away understanding clearly that everyone can make a positive contribution to making their community a better place to live.

The environmental movement has now achieved mainstream recognition, after many years of campaigning. It is generally accepted that we all need to adjust our behaviour and protect the planet as best we can from climate change. People are actively looking for ways to reduce their negative impact on the environment, and enhance the prospects of future generations. This view is now promoted in schools, in the media and, increasingly, in the boardrooms of big business. All political parties now support the concepts of fair trade, reducing carbon footprints and bringing pollution under control.

This change of awareness originated in the local actions of small groups of people who listened to the growing scientific evidence in support of the urgent need to act. They worked locally and helped others to understand that we are all interconnected – that small actions by individuals can have a significant impact on the planet.

We are now facing an equal threat to our *social environment* – our families, neighbourhoods, social networks and communities. The toxic forces that have damaged the ozone layer and threaten our supply of clean air and fresh water are placing enormous strains on the quality of our lives as social beings. Unbridled growth, rampant consumerism, individualism, careerism and greed are taking their toll on our communities. Scientific evidence supports this contention just as robustly as the research that informed the actions of the early environmentalists.

If people are to protect their social environment, action needs to be taken now before the damage to the social fabric of our society is irreversible.

Since the Industrial Revolution, we have persisted in evaluating individual happiness and our progress as a society by measuring economic growth. However, unbridled economic growth has brought significant social problems although alleviating the worst consequences of extreme poverty. This book describes how a growing number of people from a variety of backgrounds are taking action to change their personal lives and renew and protect the social environment. They are daring to step aside from a money-driven lifestyle of working, consuming and being entertained, and towards which so many others have drifted.

They have taken individual and collective responsibility for their mutual wellbeing, believing they can adapt their lifestyles, achieve more together and be happier. As a result, they now feel ***personally*** more secure, more hopeful, more in control of their lives and more fulfilled. Each is a vital part of a developing movement that is reconnecting people and valuing what they are doing to protect our ***social environment***.

This book is an invitation to join them and get involved. It will be an introduction for some readers to a whole range of different ways that people are changing the way they live. However, the main focus of this book will be on one of the most popular and fastest growing of these social innovations – ***Timebanking***.

Timebanking rewards people for their co-operation and caring, through the use of a new type of 'social money' that is put into circulation – not by banks, but by communities themselves. It provides some of the benefits of conventional money, while countering many of the social problems that conventional money creates. It is recession proof and democratic. It offers us much more appropriate indicators of individual happiness and the wellbeing of society than statistics on conventional economic growth.

Geoff Mulgan, one of this country's brightest and most influential thinkers, tells us that all great social innovations (e.g., Open University, Fair Trade, Women's Institutes, Amnesty International) have three things in common – they test assumptions, they identify threats and gaps, and they disturb the present. Timebanking and many of the other new routes to 'co-sufficiency' have certainly done all three, as this book will show. To quote Geoff: *'The courage of the ordinary people who drive forward these social innovations is contagious.'* This is a collection of their stories, of the 'ordinary miracles' in which they have shared, and the neighbourhoods they have rebuilt. Wherever possible I have used their own words and direct quotes from the people who have inspired us.

When I first heard about Timebanking, I was still working as a community organiser, using many of the techniques I had learned in the USA. However, I immediately recognised that Timebanking offered us exactly what we were all looking for – a system in which everyone could make a contribution and in which everyday human skills were recognised and valued. Better still, it offered real incentives for people to reconnect with each other. Equally important to me was the fact that the social networks that were created were shaped and controlled by local people. A chain reaction was set into motion that transformed lives; people felt safer and happier and once again a part of a supportive community.

The growth of Timebanking has far exceeded all of our most optimistic expectations; over 250 time banks have been set up in the UK already. Thousands of people of all ages, from all backgrounds and all abilities, are finding a better balance between their life as a worker and a consumer, and a new and rewarding role as a neighbour and a citizen. We have also harnessed the power of new technology to organise ourselves without the need for cumbersome, expensive and hierarchical organisations.

Our hope is that spending a few hours at your local time bank will become as normal as reading the Sunday papers.

# Chapter 1
# Our social environment

*'We are changing from a society into an audience.'* **Kurt Vonnegut**

**A CASUAL REVIEW of any of the daily newspapers would reveal a steady drip feed of reprimands and horror stories from politicians and opinion-formers about a broken Britain full of selfish people in moral decline. A picture would emerge of a society of feckless consumers demanding more and more without any regard for the consequences for others or for the planet.**

Is this a true picture of life in Britain today? Everyday experience tells me otherwise. Most of the people I come across are kind and tolerant, most of the time. We all have much to contribute to society: we have valuable skills, are capable of love, loyalty and commitment, and can take some degree of responsibility for our actions. Most people would respond positively if asked to do something specific, in some small way, which would make the world a safer and friendlier place for their family, friends and neighbours. Most people believe deep down that having solid relationships and contributing and belonging to a strong community are far better predictors of happiness and wellbeing than the brand of shoes they wear or the cost of the car they drive.

However, some powerful messages are being promoted in the media and by public services and corporations, which emphasise people's frailties and needs, rather than their strengths and capabilities.

*'Our way can often be blocked by great corporate, governmental, professional and academic institutions. They often say to us, "You are inadequate, incompetent, problematic, or broken. We will fix you".'* **John McKnight**, Community Development Expert[4]

The good news is that there is a counter-movement to all this powerful vested self-interest and negativity. This book is but a small part of a 'new compassion', a growing understanding and a belief among thousands of people across the world that we can trust ourselves and chose a better way forward – one built on caring and co-operation. This new hope for the world is eloquently expressed in the Earth Charter[5] and in this graphic representation from David Korten's book, The Great Turning[6]:

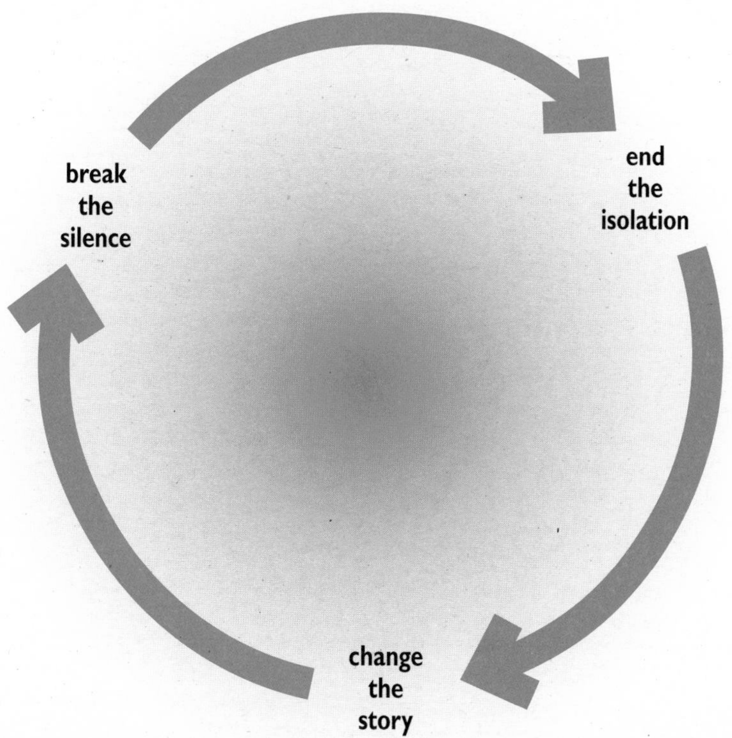

*'If you feel out of step with the way things are going in your community, nation, and the world, take heart. Your distress indicates that you are among the sane in an insane world and in very good company … The more openly we each speak our truth, the more readily others find the courage to speak theirs … we break the silence, end our isolation, and change the story in a continuous cycle that gains momentum with each iteration.'* **David Korten**, Co-founder and Chair of the Positive Futures Network

# 'Moonlighting' as a citizen

I first met Bob a couple of years ago. He is from the 'baby-boomer' generation and lives in the Forest of Dean, in Gloucestershire. He used to play rugby to a high standard and he still coaches young people. Bob is one of life's natural networkers. He enjoys using his old contacts to get free tickets to rugby matches and organises group outings to bring together people who he thinks will have things in common. When Bob talks of his childhood, he describes a different world. He remembers his home as an open house, people dropping in all day for a cup of tea and a chat.

*'We did not need a community building to have community,'* he says. Hospitality seems to have been central to everything. He remembers that when an elderly neighbour was the first to install a television set, her front room became a children's club at around 5pm each afternoon, as Bob and his friends watched Children's Hour together. But they all trooped out when her husband, George, arrived home for his tea. When George became ill, the lads would visit him; it was considered completely natural for them and other neighbours to take turns to sit with George, right up until his death. In that culture it was expected that people would be interested in each other's wellbeing. People were seldom lonely or neglected.

*'On a personal level nowadays I feel a loss of locality, of place. I've continued to be a very active and engaged person, but this is expressed through my communities of interest – work, campaigning, sports, politics and so forth, rather than through contact with my neighbours,'* said Bob. *'Logically, if I'm serious about remedying my loss of "place" I should take a back seat in respect of one or more of my communities of interest and devote time and effort to my own backyard.'*

Bob is clearly concerned by what he describes as our 'driven, workaholic, frenetic, and entertainment dependent lifestyles'. He said, *'I know that I get more R&R from time spent doing stuff with people than from solitary recreational pursuits. I wonder if my needs and preferences are the norm. I think*

*they probably are, but that lots of folk in the "rat race" do not realise that they have a choice.'*

In local communities, right up until the late 1950s, most people had a commitment to the place where they lived. This gave them a social identity, a secondary but vital and rewarding job as a citizen and a neighbour. In today's so-called 'global village', many people are losing touch with their social identity and everyday life offers few opportunities to cultivate it. Chatting with neighbours and passers-by in the areas where we live is now low on people's busy agendas. Today, most children have a television in their bedrooms and new homes are supplied with built-in Internet alcoves. People sit in cafés looking at computer screens, and on the bus, reading or listening to music, rather than connecting with those around them.

Just as the ozone layer protects our physical wellbeing, the social environment is needed to provide a protective layer for our social and psychological wellbeing. As this layer 'thins', damage is being caused to individuals and society. Undertakers report that every month there are 200 funerals in the UK that are completely unattended; the deceased, who lived amongst so many, were, in fact, completely isolated.

We are all in danger of becoming passive spectators, ever more anonymous and disconnected. I offer a vivid illustration of this point from my own family. In the 1950s, my mother organised dances in north London on Saturday nights. She would book the best dance bands and the dance halls were always packed. Across the country, dancing was by far the most popular national activity on Saturday nights. In 2010, dancing is still the most popular Saturday-night entertainment, the only difference being that people are sitting at home watching Strictly Come Dancing on television.

Global communication networks can now keep everyone in touch with the world at large, but at the same time people know increasingly less about other people in their own street. They may physically live in one shared space, but spend a great deal of home-based time mentally elsewhere, enjoying all the distractions provided by modern life – an arsenal of personal gadgets,

*'Something distinctive has been replaced by something bland; something organic by something manufactured; something definably local with something emptily placeless; something human scale with something impersonal; the result is stark, simple and brutal; everywhere is becoming the same as everywhere else.'* **Paul Kingsnorth**, Environmental Writer[7]

the seductive overtures of the entertainment industry and maybe the occasional artificial stimulant or pain-reliever. Entertainment is the present 'opium of the masses' and a very powerful drug it is too. Facebook, MySpace, Ning, Twitter, blogs and many other social-networking tools offer their users a new form of instant communication, but are resulting in a subtle but growing physical remoteness between individuals and their dispersed personal 'tribe' of family and friends.

Many older people remember the days when communities were relatively stable and unchanging, where extended families lived close together and there was always a relative on whom to call for help if needed. Local people knew each other and so had their families for generations before them. Children played in the street and parents worked and spent their leisure time nearby. Public swimming baths, playing fields, parks and woods, sports clubs, pubs, churches and corner shops were well-frequented meeting places, people felt part of a local community and the local area had an identity of its own.

People also once 'moonlighted' as citizens, gaining non-financial rewards, which were as valuable as money in providing support systems for their families. However, this local giving, receiving and reciprocating that has traditionally helped people to thrive as social beings, the favours between neighbours and hospitality toward visitors, are gradually being devalued and eroded.

## Looking out for our young

We are in danger of bequeathing a social environment to the next generation that will undermine the wellbeing and protection that they need. Research[8] shows that a civil society depends on a willingness on the part of local adults to intervene on behalf of local children; it is called 'collective efficacy'. That is why it is often said that it takes a village to raise a child. However, few people today feel that they are a part of a 'village'. The very real stresses (and joys) of life are harder to deal with (and celebrate) in a society where growing numbers of people commute to work, leaving less and less time for involvement with family and community life. Children are growing up without the care and concern of extended families or a wider community – and yet we know that the most resilient families are those that have an extended social support network. The loss of this social support, and growing isolation, has led to cases where children are suffering cruelty in their homes and neighbours are either not aware, or, if they are, hesitate to report their concerns. As I write this, the news is full of the horrific story of an 11-year-old girl in the USA, who was abducted by a known sex offender and lived for 18 years in the garden of his house in an built-up suburban residential area.

Neighbours saw her working around the house for years, later with her two children, fathered by the abductor. No-one ever approached her or possibly even passed the time of day with her. Her ordeal went on for so long because people thought acts of neighbourliness might be seen as interfering. This is an extreme case, but social isolation is putting pressure on young families, which is impacting on children every day.

Less extreme, but also worrying, research quoted in the book, The Spirit Level: Why More Equal Societies Almost Always Do Better, by Richard Wilkinson and Kate Pickett[9], suggests that in any secondary school with 1,000 students, 50 will be severely depressed, 100 will be distressed, ten to 20 will be suffering from obsessive compulsive disorder, and between five and ten girls will have an eating disorder. Adults are not doing that well either; in

*'We cannot purchase care. Care is the freely given commitment from the heart of one to another. As neighbours, we care for each other. We care for children. We care for our elders. And it is this care that is the basic power of a community of citizens. Care cannot be provided, managed or purchased from systems.'* **John McKnight**, Nova Scotia[10]

2005, doctors in England alone wrote 29 million prescriptions for anti-depressant drugs. Depression is a symptom of the 'thinning' of the social environment, but also a cause.

## Paying for services or sharing more

Another significant consequence of a colder social climate is that people are working harder and longer hours to earn more money and pay more taxes for professional strangers to carry out the tasks that they used to share with family, friends and neighbours.

Communities worked best when people pooled risk and helped neighbours out, as and when they could, knowing that when they did, others were more likely to be there for them. When local people exchanged their stories and experiences it broadened their perspectives and motivated them to do more for each other. They would have been insulted by the suggestion that they charge each other for their care or hospitality. Having time for each other brought enough rewards in itself.

## The Sufficiency of Money Game

## (adapted from The Future of Money, by Bernard Lietaer[11])

The game can be played by one or several people. There are no losers in this game; but the one who has most fun wins.

Just pretend there is no scarcity of money. It has happened by magic.

You must spend the money within your community. You can create a community of your dreams.

Then you answer these three questions:

**1. What talent would you like to develop and offer to your community?**

**2. What is the vision of your newly formed community?**

**3. Who are the other people and organisations you need to realise this vision?**

If you play this game with others, get everyone to explain their answers.

In a second round, see how your different dreams can help each other – how some of your initiatives can mesh with those of others. You will find that they strengthen each other in unexpected ways.

Some of the goals for communities that have come up when this game has been played include: quality childcare, teaching, youth mentoring, elderly care, housing repairs, infrastructure repair, environmental clean-ups, the greening of towns, arts, entertainment, music, dance, theatre, fun, transport, crime prevention and preventative healthcare.

*'We can see that there is a lot of work to be done in our communities. People have the skills and knowledge to achieve these things. Our problems are not caused by a scarcity of people or ideas. This could all be done. What is missing is money. Everyone is waiting for money.'*

**Bernard Lietaer**,
International Banker and Academic

*'The real price we pay for money is the hold that money has on our sense of what is possible - the prison it builds for our imagination.'* **Edgar Cahn**, Inventor of 'Time Dollars'[12]

But our economic system does not value community building because it does not contribute to the GDP so the money never comes. Regeneration of buildings and the employment of outside tradesmen, specialists and professional strangers increases the GDP; using local people's own capacity to look after each other without money does not even register.

## Money, as deep in our psyches as mothers' milk

Money can buy almost anything – or so we like to think. It has been a medium of exchange for centuries and has taken many forms, including beads, shells, coins, pieces of paper, electronic information held on computers and now on plastic cards. Over one million people are employed in the money industry (i.e., financial institutions) in London alone.[13] Many are earning good salaries and grand bonuses producing ever more complex financial products from which they themselves are the main beneficiaries. How ever can the planet afford them?

Money may be one of our greatest inventions, but its value rests entirely in the continuation of our shared confidence in the system that produces it. In the banking crisis of 2009, we saw what can happen if that confidence is weakened.

In December 2001, the national currency of Argentina, the pecos, collapsed and 'global barter clubs' sprung up everywhere. It was estimated that seven million people survived by sharing their time and skills and by bartering goods until the currency stabilised a few years later. People escaped from their self-imagined 'prison' – the perception that without money they could not achieve anything.

But would this happen if our monetary system collapsed? Given the present decline in community engagement, the apparent widespread selfish-

*'The simple truth is that money emerged in order*

ness (and the lack of a manufacturing base), could we survive, would people co-operate or would society disintegrate completely? Peak Oil campaigners report that young people in the UK have fewer skills than any previous generation in our history. Practical everyday skills for growing things, making things and mending things are just not being passed on through the generations.

One of the best-kept secrets in the world of high finance is that multinational corporations are now turning away from money and turning toward barter, just as they had to in Argentina. Two-thirds of all global companies use barter. They simply swap; for example, a cargo of grain for a container of cars. This reduces the risks that come from using unstable currencies and it may also (surprise, surprise) circumvent the odd tax or two. The global communication systems now available to them allow multiple participants to link up and find exchanges that suit the needs of several multinationals. Predictions are that barter will be used more and more for international trade. It would be nice to be able to report that all this enterprise was for the common good.

There are a growing number of other examples of barter, a new breed of social and local currencies that do serve the common good. 'Complementary Currencies' – Wir in Austria, Ithaca Hours and Berkshares in the USA, Talentum in Hungary, Chiemgau in Germany, Green Dollars in New Zealand, Australia and Canada, Qoin in Holland, Sane in South Africa, the Bank of Happiness in Estonia, the alternative currencies in Stroud, Brixton, Lewes and Totnes, and LETS, nearly all the world over – all aim to keep people in mind, not just profits, to trade goods locally and build a stronger community. They are growing in popularity.

Some of these 'Complementary Currencies' mimic the market and have pricing systems, just like conventional money, that set a higher value on things that are in short supply. Some are linked to national currencies and their 'bank notes' can be exchanged back and forth. Yet, all of these new currencies have a valuable part to play in protecting the social environment and connecting people to the places where they live. They all tap into the real wealth of any society – the ideas, skills and care of people – and none of them

*to facilitate human relationships - not to facilitate trade and business.'* **William Bloom**, Author[14]

exploit anyone as they do. As we continue to suffer from financial, environmental and social crises, these Complementary Currencies will, I am sure, become more visible and be used more widely. They make good sense, have the capacity to protect us from the worst effects of the free market, and offer a means by which to re-organise ourselves economically if things go completely pear-shaped.

## Timebanking is unique

Unlike other Complementary Currencies, time banks have no pricing system and they are never linked to a national currency. Their purpose is social and the focus is local.

Time banks are normally groupings of between 50 and 500 local people – informal social networks that weave together a wholesome and rewarding community life for all involved. This is precisely the original function of money – bringing people together and building relationships.

Time banks use time as a medium of exchange; one hour earns one time credit and one time credit buys one hour. Using time as a currency is in no way a new idea; in fact, in Europe it was tried as far back as the early 19th century although, according to Offe and Heinze, these early experiments 'clearly smacked of utopian socialism'.[15] Their book inspired today's Tauschringe movement in Germany.

Timebanking is an idea whose time has finally come. New time banks are opening in the UK at the rate of one a week. This has been achieved without media hype or advertising campaigns; the good news has just spread by word of mouth. It seems to sit easily with a new detectable ethos among some in society to spend less, to be more creative and friendly, and to share their knowledge and skills locally. These people now seem to understand the need for a bit more give and take – to share, make and mend, and to value what is really important: our relationships and connecting with the places where we live.

*'In my area there are numerous examples of informal gives his time to a personal fitness coach who likewise a life coach gives free sessions in return for*

Can we build on this emerging 'new order' and spread the use of this new kind of 'social' money, which is recession proof and offers people real incentives to come together, to protect and value each other and to connect again with the places where they live? For a few hours a month, can we each find the time to make use of a local currency that rewards people for co-operating, caring and sharing as automatically as conventional money rewards the competitive and the greedy?

If we do:

- We can make sure everyone is protected and safe
- We can save money and share our knowledge and skills locally
- We can provide care and mutual support without exploiting anyone
- We can tap into local know-how and connect with like-minded people
- We can have more time for family and make new friends
- We can earn a local reputation for our generosity and kindness

Can we? We can and we have.

'Timebanking taking place - a massage therapist returns the time with personal training; help with business planning.' **Jamie**, London

Timebanking is a new type of 'social' money that uses time as a medium of exchange. It is a new, safe and dynamic system that acts just like community 'loyalty points':

***You give an hour of help and earn one time credit. The person receiving your help owes one time credit. They pay back by helping someone else. The circle of care and mutual support expands; more people means more skills to share. That makes it more likely that the help you may need in the future will be there for you. You want to pay back so you help someone else …***

## How a time bank works

- Local people list all the skills and activities that they are happy to share with others
- Time credits are used as a medium of exchange; an hour's activity earns each person one time credit
- Everyone agrees to 'give and take', to both earn and spend time credits in their community
- The time credits that people earn are deposited in their individual time bank 'accounts', at the time bank
- People can spend their time credits on the skills and activities on offer from the community, or donate them to a 'community pot'
- Details of everyone's skills and of the exchanges that take place are recorded on the time bank computer and used by the 'time-broker' to match people up with the tasks that need to be done
- Everyone is an equal and valued member of the time bank

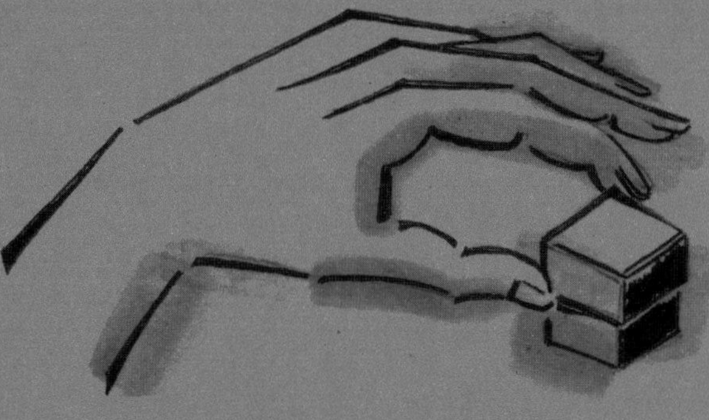

No money changes hands and people freely exchange their every day skills – skills that they often take for granted. Right now people are earning and spending their time credits at a time bank near you by giving and receiving:

Acting and auditions
Administrative support for the time bank
Adult literacy/reading lessons
Advocacy
Aerobics
Agony aunt
Agoraphobia support
Arabic lessons
Arts and crafts lessons
Assembling flat-pack furniture
Assertiveness training
Assisting with homework
Attending time bank meetings
Ambassador for the time bank
Astrology
Babysitting
Bach flower remedies
Badge making
Baking a cake
Balloon models
Barbecues
Basic legal advice
Bauble-making
Beauty care
Bee-keeping
Belly dancing
Bereavement visiting
Bicycle maintenance
Bicycle repairs
Bingo calling
Board games
Bookkeeping
Book binding
Bread-making
Breakfast and coffee mornings
Breast feeding support
Budgeting
Building furniture
Camping trips
Cantonese lessons
Carpentry
Car repairs
Car washing
Catering
Chicken-keeping advice
Childcare
Children's parties
Chinese conversation
Chocolate making
Cleaning
Cloth nappy advice
Clutter clearing
Coaching
Common sense
Companionship
Completing application forms
Composting
Computer skills
Concert tickets
Confidence building
Cookery lessons
Cooking meals
Collecting children from school
Commuters sharing skills on trains
Community cafés
Creative writing
Crime prevention advice
Crochet
Cross-country running
Crosswords
Curtain making
CV preparation
Dance classes
Databases
Day trips
Deaf awareness
Debt counselling
Design classes
Desktop publishing
Digital photography
Digging
Dinner parties
Disability Issues
DIY
DJing
Dog walking
Dog training
Downloading music and transferring to MP3
Drawing/painting
Dress advice
Dressmaking
Driving theory lessons
Driving practice
Drug information and advice
Drum lessons
Dutch language
Editing (for writers)
E-bay advice
Embroidery
Emergency response
Emotional Freedom classes
Employment readiness workshop
Emptying dishwashers
English lessons
English translation
Environmental auditing
Escorting to appointments
Escorting people on days out
Escorting to cinema
Escorting to meetings
Exercise classes
Facebook
Family law
Farsi lessons
Feng Shui consultations
Fence repairs
Festivals
Film nights
Film editing
Film/video lessons
Film and cinema club
Finding a Hebrew speaker in rural Scotland
Fishing and wildlife
Fitness training
Flower-arranging
Flu friend
Flyer design
Food foraging
Food hygiene
Food to share
Foot massage
Football coaching
Free lunch
French conversation
French lessons
Fruit picking
Fundraising
Funding advice
Gardening
Garden design
Genealogy
German lessons
Giving lifts
Glass engraving
Going for a walk with someone
Goal setting
Graphic design
Greek lessons
Greening up
Growing plants and seeds
Guest speakers
Guitar lessons
Hairdressing
Hat making
Have a go at anything!
Haymaking
Hanging curtains
Healthy eating
Heavy lifting
Help picking up litter
Heavy housework
Help with form-filling
Help with horses
Help with social events
Help with recycling
Henna tattoo
Herbal medicine
Hiking
Hindi lessons
Hire of van
Holiday accommodation
Home repairs
Hopi ear candles
Horse riding lessons
Hospital discharge visiting
Hospital visiting
Hospitality
Hot desking
House history research
House-sitting
Housework
How to secure an interview
Humorous verse
Hypnotherapy
Ice-skating
Improving local public spaces

Indian head massage
Internet skills
Interview techniques
Interior design
Ipod help
Ironing
Islamic lessons
Italian lessons
Japanese lessons
Jewellery-making
Job-hunting
Knitting
Knowledge of local government
Lacemaking
Laminating
Lawn-mowing
Leafleting
Letter writing
Lifestyle advice
Lifting heavy objects
Listening
Literacy
Loan of wheelchair
Local contacts
Local history
Local news and current affairs
Local produce
Lone parent issues
Locksmith
Loft clearing
Mail merge
Making sandwiches
Making telephone calls
Mandarin lessons
Manicures
Marketing
Market research
Maths lessons
Mattress turning
Mechanical expertise
Meditation tuition
Mentoring
Metalwork
Minibus driving
Motorbike maintenance
Motorbike repairs
Movie-making
Moving
Monitoring the Peace Garden
Mothers taking their babies to play with isolated older people
Museum tickets
Music and rhythm workshop
Music appreciation
Music course
Music lessons
Musical performance
Nature conservation
Needlecraft
Neurolinguistic programming
New neighbours
Newsletter work
Numeracy
Nutritionist advice
Odd Jobs
Oil lamp advice and repairs
Office work
Organising social events
Organisational development
Painting
Painting on pebbles
Pamper sessions
Papermaking
Parent support
Paying bills
Pedicures
Performing arts tuition
Pet care
Pet grooming
Photocopying
Photography
Piano lessons
Planning events
Plant watering
Plant swap
Playing an instrument
Poetry reading
Poetry writing groups
Poster making
Pottery
Pre/after school care
Printing
Problem sharing/solving
Proofreading
Providing local knowledge
Public speaking training
Publicity work
Puppet show
Quilting
Reading
Reading skills for children
Recording studio time
Recycling advice
Reiki
Relaxation and massage
Reminiscence
Renting holiday homes
Report writing
Research
Reports
Research on the Internet
Room hire
Running a bar
Running a café
Running a fitness club
Running a gardening club
Running a playscheme
Running errands for people
Rural cinemas
Self-expression
Self-marketing
Sewing
Sewing lessons
Shopping
Signing (BSL)
Simple painting and decorating
Singing lessons
Singing/performing to schools and social occasions
Soccer coaching for children
Somali lessons
Sorting paperwork
Spanish lessons
Sports coaching
Staffing a contact point
Stage lighting
Stage management
Stewarding at events
Storytelling
Street champion
Stress reduction
Sustainable living advice
Swahili lessons
Swedish lessons
Swimming
T'ai chi
Tarot reading
Teaching a foreign language
Teaching guitar
Teaching reading
Teaching clarinet
Teaching piano
Teaching saxophone
Telephone friend
Telephone tree
Television tuning
Theatre skills tuition
Tigrinya lessons
Training/courses
Translation
Tree planting
T-shirt printing
Tutoring (GCSE/A-level)
Typing and word processing
Ukulele workshop
Upholstery cleaning
Urdu lessons
Use of power tools
Using Photoshop
Volunteering at events
Waiting for deliveries
Walking/companionship
Walking taxis for young and old
Washing/ironing
Waxing
Wearing a Sari
Wheelchair pushing
Woodcutting
Work experience
Workshop leader
Web design
Writing advice
Window cleaning
Woodwork
Xmas tree dressing
Yoga

*'Market economics values what is scarce - not the real work of society, which is caring, loving, being a citizen, a neighbour and a human being.'*

**Edgar Cahn**[16]

Impressed? What if I were to tell you that this list represents less than half the skills and talents on offer right now from all the time banks around the country? (Many thanks, by the way, to Jon Cousins from the Avalon Time Bank for the help he gave me in compiling this sample list). We can so easily forget that every single neighbourhood in the country could produce a similar range of skills. In fact, I guarantee that there is someone a few streets away from where you live who would be able and be willing to help you out with some tasks that you find difficult or tedious. Are there things listed above that you would enjoy doing? Those interested only in making money will insist that nothing can be done without cash and try to convince you that the only help available to you is listed in the Yellow Pages.

This is simply not true.

Over the next three chapters, we'll look at a different aspect of society – personal space, social space and public space – to help you understand better how Timebanking can enhance your life. If these terms are not familiar, you might find it useful to think of society as a larger version of a local community facility – such as a local park.

A park offers a service for individuals, families and friends – times when people can enjoy some 'personal space' to just be.

However, the park facilities are also needed for use by local clubs, schools and community groups, so other times need to be set aside as 'social space'.

Finally, the park must be a 'public space' – a facility that improves quality of life for everyone and is open to all. Our lives can be similarly divided into times when we enjoy our 'personal space', maybe with family and friends; times when we inhabit a 'social space' with others in our community, be it our neighbourhood or our work setting; and, finally, times when we all belong to and help to maintain a 'public space' for the mutual benefit of everyone in society.

We may soon need to rediscover our capacity for collective action to protect our public parks. We may even take control of them as a part of the Big Society.

Read on to learn more about the ways people are responding to these challenges and threats to the wider social landscape.

# Chapter 2 In your own time: personal space

*'When a man is wrapped up in himself he makes a pretty small package.'* **John Ruskin**

**PATRICIA HAD A GOOD CAREER as a civil servant but, in her late fifties, she had to give up work when a hip replacement left her with muscle and nerve damage. *'I found myself housebound, which nearly drove me round the bend,'* she said. Luckily, she soon found her local time bank and it changed everything.**

*'It was a lifeline to the community,'* said Patricia, *'and a situation where one can give and take. I no longer feel isolated and useless.'*

Patricia trains mature people in basic IT skills – in many cases people who are on courses, but can't keep up with the other students.

*'I give extra support, one-to-one, for an hour at a time,'* she said. She has also taken up writing and performing poetry with other members of the time bank poetry group.

*'My daughter, son-in-law and three grandchildren live in Perth, Australia, and although we are in contact by email, etc., I only see them once every five years or so,'* noted Patricia.

When they heard about this situation, the time bank made her an adopted granny to the Mother & Baby group.

She said, *'I now sit in on the group from time to time and find the experience enchanting. I have had my garden fence painted by a stalwart member, lampshades installed on my high Victorian ceilings in my flat by another, and there are plans to remove a monster shrub from my garden.'*

Every month, Patricia goes to a drop-in morning at a café nearby. *'The time bank means so much to me; it has added a richness to my life, friends, a community, a feeling of being of use and of all the kindness out there. If I need assistance with anything I have only to ask.'*

The social environment is changing fast. More and more people live alongside their neighbours without knowing them. Those who can afford it are retreating into suburbia, detached houses and gated communities. People are finding it necessary to declare themselves a social-exclusion zone – to choose to exist in an 'I-cocoon'.[17]

Life hasn't always been like this and it doesn't need to be so in the future.

This chapter examines some of these forces of change that are steering people towards an existence in an 'I-cocoon'. It looks at scientific evidence that supports the need for human beings to live in communities and to connect with each other.

Patricia could have survived by switching on the TV and relying on basic care and support services from paid strangers; however, she would have had feelings of helplessness and she would have been far more at risk. People can get through most things in life if they have a circle of friends. Patricia made exactly the right choices by believing that her skills would still be of use to others. She was also prepared to accept the help she needed from others, and the practical and emotional returns have been immense.

Many older people today remember growing up in communities where the help Patricia needed would have been provided automatically by neighbours who cared, who acknowledged each other as they passed by in the street; they did favours, looked out for each other's children and left their doors unlocked. People had time for each other and people trusted each other. They each had a social identity and a local reputation. They felt relatively safe, respected and they belonged – and so did their neighbours. Children were safer playing in the streets than they would be today with a surveillance camera on every lamppost.

People have not changed that radically; they still lean towards honesty and empathy. It is the importance they place in investing in any sense of common ownership of their local neighbourhood that is slipping away. A daytime existence centred on securing an income by promoting oneself among strangers (customers), sometimes at the expense of competitors (colleagues), is tiring. It is revealing that doctors use the term 'spent' to describe the new condition of sleeplessness and malaise that people suffer as a result of their experience of modern life. There is a very real pain associated with social exclusion and the lack of a positive social identity can lead to depression and can even trigger violence. Look around the world and you will note that the more unequal societies experience higher crime rates, more addictive behaviour and worse mental health problems.

## No place like home

When we come together as a social or family group, we function according to a different set of rules. Among families and friends, people exchange gifts, borrow and lend possessions, tell stories and give away their best jokes – and feel all the better for it. On a good day, they spend time and thought making life better for each other, and regularly invite each other round for meals or other social events. In healthy families people can ask for help when they need it without believing they are a lesser person for doing so.

So why, as a society, are we now placing limits on where and when it is acceptable to be hospitable, mindful and kind? Why have we created boundaries around the circles of giving and receiving among family, friends and work colleagues, and why do we increasingly exhibit radically different behaviour to the outside world?

*'The village I live in feels typical in that there are some strong networks, but it often takes an unusual event like people helping each other clearing ice and snow, and then meeting people you haven't seen for months or even years while going sledging. People felt good about mucking in, but this hasn't been sustained.'* **Steve**, Bristol

The UK is still one of the best places in the world to live and those of us who were born here had a lucky break. People still associate this country with the image of village life, of fair play and freedom (and maybe a tad too much moaning). It helps to look a little closer at our UK 'village' and scale it down to a comprehensible level:

## If the UK were a village of 100 people

51 people would be female and 49 would be male

They would live in 43 households; 13 would be home to just one person

1 new baby would be born and 1 person would die each year

92 of the villagers would be white, 2 would be black and 1 mixed race

10 people would have been born outside the village

72 would identify themselves as Christians (only 10 would go to church)

15 would be atheists, 2 would be Muslims and 1 would be Hindu

22 people would be obese and 20 would suffer from depression

24 people would regularly drink more than their safe limits of alcohol

The villagers would have 90 television sets and 118 mobile phones

24 households would have broadband connection

30 people would have a Facebook account

16 would be at school, of which 1 would be in private education

There would be 1 teacher and 1 person in the village who was illiterate

The richest 10 people would receive 30 percent of the total income

The richest 10 people would earn more than the poorest 50 combined

The 80 adults would share a personal debt of £2.4m (£30,480 each)

There would be 44 cars, 2 motorbikes, 13 cats and 13 dogs

56 villagers would give regularly to charity and there would be 3 vegetarians

The villagers would generate 163kg of waste every day, of which just 47kg would be put out for recycling.

*From The Independent, 21 July 2009*

# Us and them

The free market operates around profit and loss – one person's profit necessitates another person's loss. The market not only thrives when it meets our needs but, more particularly, when it creates them. Businesses and 'social entrepreneurs' now feel obliged to look into almost every area of human life to ask: How can I make money out of this? There are profits to be made from families whose breadwinners are busy working away from home, so need to buy in services for their family. A recent estimate of the cost of the outsourcing of family tasks was over £18 billion a year.[18]

When people make a comfortable living and accumulate possessions over and above those they need to survive, they instinctively feel the need to defend them against what can seem a hostile world. 'Out there' becomes a dangerous place and this view is perpetuated by a weak social environment – a way of life that inhibits people from connecting with those around them. This, in turn, creates an 'us and them' mentality, which is easier to assume when we have a weak social identity and little connection to the place we live. How have we let this happen?

The outside world is presented through a filter of 24-hour television, radio, newspapers, websites and mass-marketed magazines that claim to be reporting on life as it is but, in fact, choose to shock and entertain with dramas, sensationalism and controversy in order to sell more product.

Repeated exposure to all this can lead people to project this negative commentary on 'life' onto the place where they live.

# Isolation

Combine this with a lack of opportunity to freely mix with others and it is easy to understand how facts and reality become confused with fears and suspicions generated by the media. The fear of crime and suspicions about strangers far outweigh actual experiences of being a victim of abuse or crime. However, people still keep their doors locked and their windows shut, becoming ever more isolated. This actually means greater exposure to risk; predators seek out the isolated as there is less chance of being observed and more chance of manipulating them.

Irrational fears are making people curtail their lives as responsible adults. I was talking to a neighbour recently and he told me that his young son was being bullied on his way home from school. I suggested that he went to collect his child from school and had a look around to find out what was going on.

*'I can't hang around the school,'* he replied. *'They will think I am up to no good.'*

# Individualism

A culture of celebrity worship and the popularity of reality television is turning lots of very ordinary people into newsworthy objects. 'Reality' television is clearly not reality at all, yet people are aspiring to be like 'celebrities', despite the fact that these lives are caricatured and exaggerated. It may be that they think that celebrity will bring with it impunity, when they see the excesses of their favourite celebrities being excused and indulged.

Bill McKibben, in his book Deep Economy: Economics as if the World Mattered[19], drew attention to the fact that so many quiz and reality television shows in the USA are constructed in order to support individualism and consumerism. They may be reflecting the audience's preferences, but the subtle impact on their culture is not healthy.

*Average time spent shopping per week in the USA:*
*Average time spent playing with children per week in the USA:*

The same is true in the UK. In Big Brother, for example, 'house mates' used to conspire to eject each other until the winner was left alone in the house with all the money.

This normalisation of individualism extends to the workplace, where people are spending less time together working in groups and more time alone with computerised machines in offices and factories. The world of commerce has become so competitive that people feel they have to work longer hours in jobs they are finding increasingly stressful. By way of compensation, they feel they deserve treats for themselves, for their children and even for their pets: things they can't really afford and don't really need. Pleasure is confused with happiness and, as with any addiction, it needs constant feeding.

## Convenience for an 'I-cocoon'

Perhaps the most obvious example of where the march of individualism and consumerism has impacted badly on the local social environment is the arrival of the supermarket. The supermarkets offer more choice and cheaper food all in one place. They offer convenience, accessibility, free parking and long opening hours. However, for the local area, this arrival meant specialist shops closing, money going out of the community, local wages being driven down and people accepting packaged food that had been grown and prepared elsewhere. A chilling statistic is that in the 1950s there were nearly a quarter of a million food shops in the UK; but, in 1997, there were only just over 35,000. Even more chill-provoking is the claim that another three Walmart stores open somewhere in the world every week.

*6 hours.*

*40 minutes.'* **David Boyle**, Author and New Economics Foundation Consultant[20]

Soon the corporate machine will know more about us than we know about each other. Our financial records and shopping habits already provide them with detailed profiles of us. From this information stores can stock their shelves appropriately to maximise sales. Customers can then go in and buy what they want without having to talk to anyone. This is an ideal shopping environment for an 'I-cocoon': on average, each person has ten conversations at a farmers' market, at a supermarket only one.[22]

*'In order for the global consumer economy to progress we must cease to be people who belong to neighbourhoods, communities, localities. We must cease to value the distinctiveness of where we are. We must become consumers, bargain-hunters, dealers on a faceless, placeless international trading floor. We must cease to identify with our neighbourhoods, our landscape, and our locality, or to care much about it. We must become citizens of nowhere.'* **Paul Kingsnorth**[21]

## 'Urban Law'
## Alison Hawthorne Deming[23]

Rush hour and the urban outflow pours
across the Million Dollar bridge. I wait
for the walk-light, cross traffic-slight but
caution's the rule when the city roars
toward all its separate homes. I get
the sign, a little electric man, and step
into the street. A woman turns into
my lane, bearing down, eye-contact,
and still she guns it until I stare and
shake my head in disbelief at her
ferocity. She slows begrudged to let
me pass, runs down the window of her Saab
and shouts, 'Why don't you wait for the light?'
and flips me the bird. I feel weepy like
a punished child, mind sinking to lament,
What's wrong with the human race? Too many
of us, too crowded, too greedy for space –
we're doomed, of course, so I head for coffee
and a muffin, walking sad and slow on
the return. I'm waiting again to cross,
picking fingersful of muffin from the
paper sack and watching the phalanx of
cars race by, not even a cell of a
thought in my mind that I might jump the change,
when a man who's got the green stops,
an executive wearing a crisp white
shirt and shiny red tie, and he raises
his palm to gesture me safely across,
making all the cars behind him wait while
I walk, and together at rush hour that
man and I redeem the whole human race.

*'Compassion and altruism have never found their place as significant terms in modern psychologies. And the apparent realism of all the self-interest stories - the accounts of human nature as essentially self-seeking and self-satisfying - have made the kindness stories soppy, or wishful, or simply the province of the religious ... ordinary kindness is not a manipulative bribe or a magical cure, but a simple exchange ... kindness comes from a revived awareness of something that is already felt and known ... kindness is a continual temptation in everyday life that we resist. Not a temptation to sacrifice ourselves, but to include ourselves with others.'* **Adam Phillips**, Psychoanalyst, and **Barbara Taylor**, Historian[24]

Little things, such as avoiding eye contact on a crowded bus or dropping a piece of litter in the street can add to people's feelings of detachment. A smile of recognition to a stranger or a random act of kindness can brighten the day of everyone who experiences them.

Advertisers and marketing people understand the influencing power of human qualities like kindness, compassion, generosity and fair play.

They promote them, but only to sell their products. They offer them as guaranteed outcomes if you make the right consumer choices. Among my junk mail this morning was a bright blue leaflet from 'The Real Local Heroes, great offers from businesses you love'. I am unsure whether the shopkeepers and tradespeople that were advertised offer me value or a good service, but I am sure they are not my idea of heroes nor are they likely to become the objects of my love.

## Including strangers

Elaine describes herself as a foreign young woman living alone in London.

She said, *'When I bring someone back to my flat for the first time, I often explain the ups and downs of where I live, concluding that the best thing about my "hood" is its people. There is my elderly neighbour downstairs, who will have discreetly checked out any new visitor before they've made it through my door! My next-door neighbour Debbie and I help each other out with bits and pieces. I go to a house down the road where I take a yoga class for free! Sometimes I teach maths to the yoga instructor's son, who loves hanging out with me and getting "messy": planting seeds or baking. His mum sometimes sends round curries with chapati. When I'm feeling down and lonely, a text offering chicken curry really cheers me up!*

*'Jenny, Debbie and I all share food, especially when there's baking going on, and help each other out if someone is sick or needing help with something.'*

Other people have told Elaine that having a relationship with neighbours is unusual for London.

*'Maybe it's because I'm a strong believer in community cohesion or maybe it's because I love cooking and exchanging food!'* Elaine said. *'I do value love and healthy relationships above all else. To me this little network provides me with a lot of safety, some support and of course friendship.'*

She grew up in a small, close-knit community, which meant that a lot of support and care was available. Because everyone knew each other, there wasn't any petty crime and people felt safe to reach out a helping hand to one another.

*'The first time I approached a time bank was when my fridge broke down about four years ago. Unfortunately my local time bank didn't have someone who could help on their books, but I was quite keen to earn credits by translating and helping kids with homework,'* she said. Elaine now gives a couple of hours when she wants to and receives valuable experiences that have helped her in many

different ways with her career.

She noted, *'In the area where I work, a time bank could help break down social boundaries and perhaps tackle barriers for individuals to move within different social groups. One day, when Timebanking grows bigger, I would like to be able to go to a beauty salon and pay in time credits. I would love to be able to buy original arts and crafts with time credits and the opportunity to be creative with textiles and sell these for time credits.'*

Unfortunately, these days, a new local resident from another country offering to lend a hand is quite likely to be met with wariness and they can even represent a threat if perceived as too 'different'. Hospitality is an essential ingredient of a civil society and the UK has long been noted for its willingness to be both welcoming and tolerant. The Victorians called it 'open-heartedness'. Will historians look back on the early 21st century as the age of cold-heartedness? Or the beginning of a new social warming?

If they are going to define us as warm, then things need to change quickly; at present, our young people are being influenced by the way our society appears to value competition over co-operation and compassion, as these figures from Richard Layard's book, Happiness,show:[25]

| Percentage of children aged 11 to 15 agreeing that *'Most of the students in my class(es) are kind and helpful'* | |
|---|---|
| Switzerland | 81% |
| Sweden | 77% |
| Germany | 76% |
| Denmark | 73% |
| France | 54% |
| USA | 53% |
| Russia | 46% |
| UK | 43% |

## All tomorrow's children

Many thinkers have pointed out that how we treat our children and relate to our neighbour's children today will shape the world that we will find ourselves living in tomorrow.

Shannon was 13 years old when she joined her local time bank. She said, *'My mum thought it would be good for me to learn more about the value of time!'*

She had flute lessons, which she could not have afforded any other way.

*'I had a 30-minute flute lesson every week for over a year. To repay the time, I delivered flyers to houses and did karate demonstrations at different time-bank social events,'* she said. She also helped out with pet care for someone who went away for a month.

*'They had eight cats, one dog, four ducks, eight chickens and a turkey. It was fun chasing them around in the evening to get them back into their hutches,'* said Shannon.

She has met 'loads of people' through the time bank and said, *'They all seem to care about me and look after me. It's as if they're family; it's great.'* She has been on numerous day trips and to several theatre productions, and has been able to pay for it all with time credits.

Shannon said, *'My mum even booked the soft play area at the Gateway for my birthday party, for me and ten friends, all for time credits. It was great fun and it didn't cost a thing.'*

Shannon is hard to stop when she gets going, talking about what she has been up to at her time bank. She said, *'I have done so much that I wouldn't have been able to do over the last three years. I've even had my bike repaired and attended crafts session, swapped books in the book swap, painted pots and planted bulbs at the "time barbecue", plus lots and lots more. I can't remember it all. I've been involved in that much.'*

*'To decide to notice, rather than ignore it, when a neighbour is losing it with her kid and offer to baby-sit twice a week. This is not interference. Getting between a ball player and a ball is interference. The ball is inanimate. Presuming children to be their parent's sole property and responsibility is, among other things, a handy way of declaring problem children to be someone else's problem, or fault, or failure. It's a dangerous remedy; it doesn't change the fact that somebody else's kid will ultimately be in your face demanding now with interest what they didn't get when they were smaller and had simpler needs. Maybe in your face means breaking and entering, or maybe it means a savings and loan scam. Children deprived - of love, money, attention or moral guidance - grow up to have large and powerful needs … they were all once somebody's baby; how on earth did they learn to be so isolated and selfish?'* **Barbara Kingsolver**, Author[26]

## We are social animals

Sharing more of our personal time with others is sensible, rewarding and warming and it is precisely what we were designed to do. Human beings are hard-wired to co-operate. Anthropologists categorise us as 'co-operative breeders'. Our young need to be protected for many years after birth and so we form attachments and share in their care. There is a deep reciprocal exchange of love between a mother and her baby that forms the building blocks for all future relationships. It is the nature and quality of these interdependent relationships with family, friends and neighbours that once determined if we were to survive as a species, and now dictates where real happiness and contentment in life is to be found.

In her article, 'The Selfless Gene', environmental biologist Olivia Hudson[28] gives those of us who believe in the possibility of a new compassion (The Great Turning) ever more reason to be optimistic. She asserts that friendliness has a genetic underpinning and is as 'primal as ferocity', and says: *'Indeed, the ability to adjust our behaviour to fit a given social environment is one of our main characteristics, yet it is so instinctive we don't even notice it, let alone consider it worthy of remark. But its implications are profound and hopeful. It suggests that we can, in principle, organise society so as to bring out the best facets of our complex, evolved natures.'*

Sue Townsend, author of the Adrian Mole books, has made it something of a personal mission to remind us whenever she can that the vast majority of people are actually looking for an opportunity to demonstrate their best selves. She also shares our optimism about change being possible: *'We are on the cusp of something significant, because if it goes on this way what kind of world are we going to be living in? We're going to be paranoid, fearful, isolated.'*

In part of his speech in Nova Scotia, John McKnight very neatly and succinctly articulated the first steps that we need to take to be citizens: *'First, we see what we have – individually, as neighbours and in this place of ours. Second, we know that the power of what we have grows from creating new*

*'Even if we manage to survive what most people are worrying about - global warming, emergent diseases, rogue viruses, meteorites crashing into earth - will we still be human thousands of years down the line. By that I mean in the way we currently define ourselves. The reason our species has managed to survive and proliferate to the extent the six billion people currently occupy the planet has to do with how readily we can learn to co-operate when we want to. And our capacity for empathy is one of the things that made us good at doing that. The capacity for empathy is uniquely well developed in our species, so much so that many people believe that along with language and symbolic thought, it is what makes us human ... During the first years of life, within the context of early relationships with mothers and other committed caretakers, each individual learns to look at the world from someone else's perspective.'* **Sarah Blaffer Hrdy**[27]

*connections and relationships among and between what we have. Third, we know that these connections happen when we individually or collectively act to make connections – they don't just happen by themselves.'*

We need a new and safe framework for people to make these connections, an information system about what people can offer and what others need and a means to encourage people to act. We need a system that values everyone's contribution equally and rewards them when they share their skills, mix freely and relearn the art of hospitality.

When you join a time bank you join a counter-movement to the marketers and advertisers whose job it has been to convince you to become a passive consumer of their products. Timebanking is an ideal tool to create a new culture and explore fresh possibilities.

The new Coalition Government would seem to be in full support. Talk of 'Big Society' and a 'people power revolution' is encouraging. Things could hardly have continued as they were. New Labour had given local authorities the hopeless and thankless task of controlling us all. Ludicrous guidelines around safety were issued seemingly daily, like the one to public park officials warning them to view any man seen walking alone in the park as suspicious and to follow and question him. This was such an infringement of the rights of citizens to occupy personal space in a public park that the guidelines were widely ridiculed and quickly withdrawn.

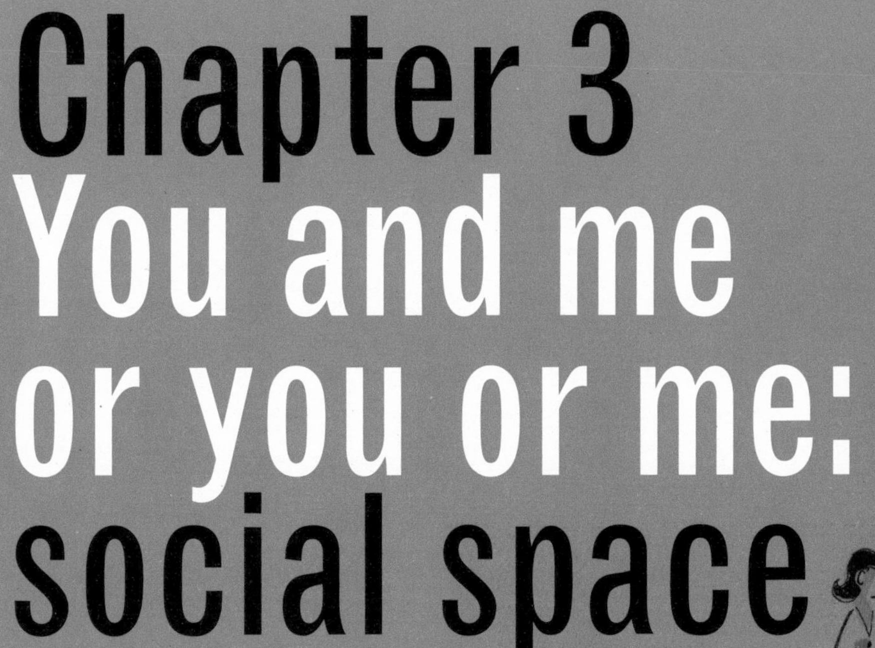

# Chapter 3
# You and me or you or me: social space

*Man is sensible that his own interest is connected with the prosperity of society and that his happiness, perhaps the preservation of his existence, depends on its preservation.'* **Adam Smith**

*'The way we live is eroding our capacity for deep, sustained, perceptive attention - the building blocks of intimacy, wisdom and cultural progress.'*

**Maggie Jackson,**
Journalist and Author[29]

**IN 1976, BUCKMINSTER FULLER, a 'social architect', claimed that as a human family we had crossed a critical threshold. In his seminal lecture in London, he predicted that, *'We are doing so much with so much less now everyone can have everything they need – but it will take 50 years for us to realise it.'***

His belief was that we already had the technology and the know-how for everyone to live a good life at no-one else's expense. There were the machines to mass-produce the goods and enough socially aware and sensible people to see that things were distributed fairly. But, just as he predicted, people have still not worked out what this could mean for them and for society. He was aware of all the time- and labour-saving devices around at the time, but even he didn't foresee an equal amount of skill and energy being invested in marketing 'time-filling' devices like MP3 players, flat-screen televisions, DVDs, CDs, laptops, mobile phones and games consoles. The gadgets we have brought into our lives keep us more distracted than even he could have imagined. The executives who market these gadgets talk publicly about how their new product is going to achieve a specific percentage of both 'market share' and 'mind share'. In other words, they calculate the extent to which their latest toy will entrap the minds of their customers.

At least some people are getting a little bit angry at all the waste. More people seem to be aware of the need to step out of the repetitive cycle of working, shopping and being entertained. Most of us, at least, know which products are purposely manufactured to have a limited life; whether we will ever stop buying them, I am not so sure. Changing fashions still mean that clothes and other goods are being needlessly discarded. Simulated pressures to upgrade things make us discontent with what we have and we are now a society that manufactures needs, not goods; the goods are made more cheaply somewhere else. And we have more goods than we need.

*'What I'd like to see happening in my street is a kind of "tool" time bank. When I think of how many lawnmowers, drills and carpet-washers there must be sat in sheds, how many separate internet connections there probably are, I think, what a waste of resources. Our street has about 40 houses and we could easily share maybe five lawnmowers. Everyone could pay in time to use them.'* **Sarah**, Stroud

## The rich get richer and the poor get poorer

More than 30 years have passed since the Buckminster Fuller lecture but people's desire for conspicuous consumption continues to cloud their reason. This means that, as predicted, the few have continued to profit and the majority have remained disempowered. Our social divisions have widened. In 1974 (excluding housing), the poorest half of the population owned 12 percent of the personal wealth. In 2009, they owned just 1 percent.[30] In 2006, as reported by the FSA, 43 percent of people have no savings at all.

As Ian Angell, from the London School of Economics, wrote in The Independent, the early warning signals of an even more unequal and troubled society to come are loud and clear: *'The main problem of the future will be the glut of unnecessary people who will be irrelevant to the needs of corporations and therefore will be uneducated, untrained, ageing and resentful … the slow redistribution of wealth to which we came accustomed after World War II is already rapidly reversed, so the future is one of inequality … The world belongs already to the global corporation.'*

If you think that this looks to you like scaremongering, then you haven't heard yet about Public Realm Agreements.[31] In Liverpool, the City Council has given a development company a 250-year lease on a 42-acre city centre site, including a public park and 34 streets. They have signed over our rights to enter public streets. They will be patrolled, not by the police, but

*'Operating in a world of instant communication with minimal social*

by private security guards, who will enforce rules set down by the property company. These public streets, and many others, will no longer belong to the people (or Her Majesty), and entry will be denied to anyone who isn't shopping. Public Realm-type Agreements have long been used in the USA; there, access to public streets is denied outside of shop opening hours. In short, people without the right credit rating can be stopped from walking along a public street. A closed environment for 'I-cocoons' of high-earning shoppers is being developed at the heart of the once-proud people's City of Liverpool. I am told that Public Realm Agreements are increasingly being used now in London and in many other cities.

## It wasn't meant to be like this

Adam Smith, the creator of the theory of free market economics, believed that exploitation of others would be held in check by the social structures that guided everyone's behaviour at that time. He wrote: *'For the rich, the reward system would be balanced between the pleasure of self-gain and the civic pride of serving others. By these means the most powerful citizens would be limited in their greed.'*

Such social constraints may have been in place then and they may still be relevant in smaller, more coherent societies. In the global marketplace, they are weak, if not impotent.

We are inflicting damage both on our social fabric and on the planet.

The activities of multinational corporations and financial institutions represent a reckless departure from all that is sensible and sustainable, yet they appear incapable of changing direction.

In his book ***You Are Therefore I Am***[33], Satish Kumar eloquently reminds us that we depend on the earth and on each other:

*tethers our engines of commerce and desire became turbo charged.'*

**Peter Whybrow**, Neuroscientist[32]

*'The Industrial Revolution, scientific discoveries and technological inventions have created the illusion that we, the human race, are the rulers, that we can take nature's laws into our own hands, and do what we like with them … This is human arrogance at its worst. As a result we have turned the abundant bounty of natural gifts into scarcity. Time is infinite, yet we have turned it into a limited commodity. We have reduced the Earth, our planet, our home, to a battlefield where we are competing and fighting for materials, markets and power … We can take the road to ruin. We can drive over the abyss. Or we can turn towards ecology … Like the Chinese in the Middle Ages, who discovered gunpowder but decided to use it only for fireworks, we can be wise and say enough is enough.'*

# Total productive system of an industrial society

Official market economy, all cash transactions

*GNP-monetised half of cake*

Top two layers monetised, officially measured GNP generates all economic statistics (15% 'underground' illegal, tax-dodging)

'Private' sector production, employment, consumption, investment, savings

GNP 'private' sector rests on

Defence, state and local government, 'public' sector infrastructure (roads, maintenance, sewers, bridges, subways, schools, municipal government

Cash-based 'underground economy' tax dodges

GNP 'public' sector rests on

*Non-monetised productive half of cake*

Lower two layers non-monetised altruism, sharing 'counter-economy' subsidises top two GNP cash sectors with unpaid labour and environmental costs absorbed or unaccounted, risks passed to future generations

"Sweat-equity', do-it-yoursel, bartering. Social, familial, community structures, unpaid household and parenting, volunteering, sharing, mutual aid, caring for old and sick, home-based production for use, subsistence agriculture

Social co-operative counter-economy rests on

MOTHER NATURE

Natural resource base - absorbs costs of pollution, recycles wastes if tolerances not exceeded. GNP sectors 'external' costs hidden (toxic dumps, etc.)

Nature's layer

*Hazel Henderson, Futurist and Economic Iconoclast, illustrates how the monetised layers of her 'cake' rest on top of and depend on non-monetised but equally productive 'sweat equity' and 'Mother Nature'. We need to recognise and strengthen the contribution made by the bottom two layers (the physical and social environments), without which all above it – our global suicide economy – will surely soon collapse in on itself.*

In her book, Hazel Henderson remains optimistic and believes that we are moving into a new 'Attention Economy' where time and attention will become as valuable to us as money. She says that people will reject the 'mediocracies' they live in 'where a few media moguls now control the attention of billions of people'. They will choose new challenges, personal growth and a better quality of life. They will want less money and more time, less stress and more peaceful and fulfilling times spent with family, friends and the local community. She believes that people are becoming more self aware and socially responsible and soon it will be much harder for *'governments to hype wasteful, goods-based GDP growth in the global economy without measuring toxic wastes, resource depletion, shrinking water supplies, polluted air, unsafe streets, drugs, poverty and global epidemics'*. People, she believes, will become concerned once again about the need for more caring, more prevention and more individual and community wellbeing and demand new 'social' seals of approval for cleaner, greener products - much like a more formal re-introduction into society of the informal social constraints that existed in communities in Adam Smith's day.

## No friends of ours

The super-rich minority are exploiters of nature and the good nature of the majority of people. But some people continue to aspire to be like them and envy their money and their conspicuous consumption. This may cause these people to work hard, but it distorts their values and weakens social constraints on selfish and individualistic behaviour. Out of the rat race and into a rat chase. This can be detected in the attitude of the ruling elite. Politicians here in the UK have recently been caught with their hands in the till; business leaders continue to empty the till at every opportunity, and all of the tills are being made in China.

*'People rely increasingly on money as a criterion of value. What is more expensive is considered better. The value of a work of art can be judged by the price it fetches. People deserve respect and admiration because they are rich. What used to be a medium of exchange has usurped the place of fundamental values ... Society has lost its anchor.'*

**George Soros,**
Currency Speculator[35]

# A parallel economic system

There are two economic systems that have always run side by side. Economists and politicians recognise and take into account only the market economy and ignore a parallel economic system that seems to be completely invisible to them. Yet we all depend on it and businesses could not function without it. We have taken it for granted for years, and it is urgently in need of some investment.

The word 'economics' derives from the ancient Greek word for 'management of the household': Oikonomia. The household was the core economic system and it included all sorts of exchange networks between families, neighbours and the wider community. Neva Godwin, an environmental economist, still calls it the 'core economy' (it is often referred to as the non-market economy), and it is as crucial to our lives as it ever was. Every community has a vast resource of practical skills, energy, caring, compassion, experience and common sense waiting to be utilised.

One of the most popular Timebanking slogans is: ***'We have what we need if we use what we have.'***

This thinking has been further inspired by Lynne Twist's Principle of Sufficiency:[36] *'When you let go of trying to get more of what you don't really need – which is what we are always trying to get more of – an enormous amount of energy is freed up to make a difference with what you have. When you make a difference with what you have – it expands.'*

The core economy operates just like this – the more it is used and new connections are made, the more it expands. It runs primarily on relationships – emotional ties, favours, mutual respect, and give and take – on hospitality and spontaneity, on feeling good when we are of use to others, and on feeling safe because we know there are others around who care.

But there are gaps opening up in the core economy that will be as damaging to people's social and psychological wellbeing as the holes in the ozone layer are to the planet and our physical wellbeing. The core economy provides the social glue that holds families and communities together and we are only beginning to realise what we are losing with its gradual weakening and increasing ineffectiveness.

*'Those universal capacities that have enabled our species to survive and evolve: our ability to care for each other, to learn from each other, to stand up for what is right and oppose what is wrong. In terms of rebuilding the core economy those capacities are literally priceless. Yet we take them for granted in roughly the same way we took clean air and clean water and the ozone layer for granted, until the toxicity we unleashed jeopardised our health and survival … After all, families are supposed to function; children are supposed to be resilient, trust is supposed to be present whenever intentions are good; people do what they are supposed to do; collective self-interest can be counted on to advance public wellbeing. And altruism, like the ozone layer, will always shield us from destructive selfishness.'*

**Edgar Cahn**[37]

## A free ride for the market economy

Another unrecognised function of the core economy is that it acts as a prop for the market economy. Alvin Toffler, in his book Revolutionary Wealth[38] points out that, for example, when parents pay for private tutors for their children's education they are subsidising the state education system. When retired baby-boomers care for their parents and for their grandchildren they are subsidising both the social-care and the childcare systems. Mothers provide the vast majority of medical care, not doctors or nurses. When friends and neighbours rally round in emergencies, when volunteers help out in schools, when people put out their dustbins and sort out items to recycle, when self-help groups look out for one another, and when people run street parties and festivals that contribute so much to community cohesion – they are all subsidising the market, for free.

## Who cares?

Bee became a mini-celebrity in south London when she won the right for her pet dog to be recognised as one of her most valuable and important formal 'carers'. She was also a wonderful and enthusiastic spokeswoman for Time-banking and she and her dog appear regularly on our promotional videos – much to everyone's delight! It has not always been like that.

Before she joined her local time bank she told me, *'I was very lonely living on my own, with severe mental health problems in the form of an eating disorder which had made me not at all well. I didn't know what to do. I did not go out and didn't have many friends. I now go out and about and would not be without my daily walk down to the shops to see all my mates in the community and have a drink in a couple of cafés. I would like to recommend other people to join a time bank. I have a higher self-esteem and am far more confident; and, as a side effect, I have gained a little weight.*

*'I have been lucky enough to have had a time-bank member put up a shelf for me and one other member came and dug over my garden. I have attended training sessions in massage and jewellery-making, and a women's pampering day.'*

But the rewards have by no means been only one way. Bee produced audio cassettes of all different types of people reading poems and other texts for visually impaired members of the time bank, and she also produced a short booklet of poems for GP surgeries, as *'an alternative to reading old, out-of-date, glossy magazines'*. She has also been the time bank's official events photographer.

She said, *'I have held coffee mornings at my house once every other month for over a year now and those who come enjoy it and lots of networking is done. I also attend the monthly coffee morning that the time bank holds at the café. Time-bank members have given me friendship and advice; they take me to meetings and two have come with me to the supermarket, as I am very, very bad at doing my own shopping. It is so good just to know that someone is there sometimes to talk to.'*

Bee touched many people; she was a larger-than-life character, but with a frail body. Bee recently died unexpectedly before having a chance to see this book. I think she would have been proud to see one of her favourite pastimes, Timebanking, celebrated in print, and I can imagine her making sure everyone knew about it. Bee taught us all that we should never be afraid of being ourselves and for that alone she will live on in our memories. She was our first Timebanking star.

A 2001 Home Office Citizenship Survey estimated that volunteering contributed the equivalent of £36 billion to the UK economy. People looking after sick or disabled relatives provide care worth an estimated £23 billion a year, according to the Public Accounts Committee. There are an estimated 6 million unpaid carers. I am reliably informed that there are legions of young carers burdened with immense caring responsibilities – so many, in fact, that if we knew the true picture it would constitute a national disgrace.

As mentioned, Alvin Toffler, believes that the market owes an immense amount to the core economy, as parents, friends and neighbours are, after all, the main agents of child development and socialisation. Each new generation is rehearsed with hours of free tuition from their families so that they may enter the existing social order and its economy. He asks us, part in jest, to consider what it would cost multinational corporations if their executives were not toilet-trained. How could businesses function if the streets were not safe for their staff and customers? But it is only the people living there who can prevent anti-social activities and keep our communities safe, not the police. There was a time when police and communities respected and trusted each other, and information and intelligence flowed freely between them. There was a time when crimes were solved, disputes were resolved by early interventions and offenders were caught. Corners may have been cut, but everyone knew the score. Many years ago, my uncle Jack ran a large pub in Kentish Town that was frequented by many a local villain. I visited once and was curious to know why there were no customers. I was told that it was the Police Benefit dinner and dance that evening.

*'Ah,'* I declared, *'all the locals are out and about getting up to mischief then.'*

*'No way,'* replied my uncle, *'they are all at the Police dinner and dance.'*

## Price or value?

No pricing system is needed in the core economy when it works well; everyone contributes what they can, when they can and is valued equally for their part in keeping their family or community healthy and fully functioning. Healthy communities are built on the giving and receiving of care, encouragement, kindness, compassion and respect; these are valuable qualities, some say priceless assets. If the core economy is to thrive again people have to place a higher value on these human qualities rather than allow the marketplace to devalue them just because they are in plentiful supply.

# Another anthropologist's view

**Polly Wiessener is Co-Chair of the Board of TimeBanks USA. She works at the Department of Anthropology at the University of Utah and has studied tribal people in Papua, New Guinea, and the Bushmen of Southern Africa for many years.**

For tens of millennia, the core economy stood alone in providing social, emotional and economic micro-credit to assist members in realising their aspirations or buffering their losses from the cradle to the grave. Today it produces care for children, families and seniors, safe and vibrant neighbourhoods, community, democracy and civil society. Problems in the core economy can be attributed to many factors, for example, individuality, materialism, mobility and changing gender roles, but central among these is the high transaction costs of traditional core economies. For example, locating and evaluating assets involved in gathering information from personal networks and experimentation. Those with narrow networks were at a great disadvantage; in-group out-group membership inhibited the flow of information. Searches were time-consuming and became ever more so with increasing mobility. Negotiation of sharing and reciprocity was complex in exchanges that were often governed by terms of need and ability to fill it. Because sharing and reciprocity are subject to free riding, monitoring and enforcement costs were high – gossip and the exertion of social sanctions. A core economy with such high transaction costs no longer meets the exigencies of today nor the needs of a society valuing privacy.

Timebanking greatly reduces search costs through providing a database that lists assets as well as when and where they are available, a significant advantage in highly mobile communities. Everybody in the pool has an equal information advantage and opportunity to post assets. The database and the co-ordinators hold memory of successful interaction to be repeated, and unsuccessful ones to be avoided. Equality of an hour of banked currency, time, eliminates negotiations. Receivers get services that they need when they really need them; givers can build reputation and store hours for times of need. Finally, monitoring and enforcement come easily in Timebanking; since a limited number of hours can be taken out of the bank before the receiver must replenish his or her account, it is difficult to free ride. In a nutshell, Timebanking empowers people to foster relationships of reciprocity and trust, build positive reputations and tap into the assets of all members; it can serve as long-term care insurance or social and economic microfinance. It has the power to change human relations from charity to parity, from anonymity to community, from dependency to sufficiency and to bring the alienated home.

# Public goods

The core economy produces a range of 'public goods': safe neighbourhoods, care for the elderly and the marginalised, social justice, environmental clean ups and recycling, a place for healthy children to belong to, public health, community events and celebrations and, not least, a basis for a working democracy.

Such public goods are produced and preserved when people link with the like-minded and share skills, experiences and contacts across loose social networks in the neighbourhoods where they live. They are products from which all may benefit, whether or not they helped to create them and are passed on, in good shape or run down, to future generations.

Unfortunately our legal system and the importation of a compensation culture from the USA is hindering the production of public goods. When things go wrong, appeals are made to outside authorities; they are no longer handled locally. People are being convinced that the correct response to a local issue is litigation, even though time and again lawyers are the only ones to benefit. A civil rights lawyer himself, Edgar Cahn, the inventor of time dollars, reminds us that lawyers are good at picking fights but not as good at coming up with long-term solutions.

Cahn said: *'I can keep a person from being evicted, but I can't make where they are living a place I would want to live and raise my children. That means I have a choice. My life can be a series of well-intentioned but inconsequential victories that make no real difference to the life of others. Or I can acknowledge that I need what my clients can do in their community as badly as they need what I can do in the courtroom. If my work is to have meaning I need to acknowledge that I need them as badly as they need me. Time dollars supply the mechanism. They have reciprocity built in. I help you; you give back by helping someone else; and sooner or later down the line that comes back to me.'*

Someone who knows what he can do for his community is Keith, who lives in Derwent. He is in his early fifties, and married with five grown-up children and eight grandchildren. He originally joined the time bank after his wife told him it would be 'right up his street'.

He said, *'I first did light gardening jobs as I had a lot of experience'*, and, since then, he has been the backbone of his time bank, offering people his skills in fencing, DIY, pet care, transportation, and tool repair and sharpening.

Keith said, *'In return, I have received help with my ironing, cleaning, pet care and complementary therapy; I have also attended coffee mornings, training sessions, social events and gone to the theatre and on day trips.'* Keith told me that he had made a lot of new friends and had benefitted considerably from the time bank.

*'I am always busy thinking about the next exchange taking place,'* he noted. Teaching some of his many skills to other members is now his mission, so that *'others can take over from me when I am unable to carry on physically. This way the time bank will continue indefinitely and if all members can do the same, then the whole community will benefit.'*

## No win, no fee, we lose

When I returned from the USA, I used many of the community organising techniques I had learned to protect people's rights by holding to account uncaring, negligent or unresponsive officials and professionals.

For example, Mark Gale (my dear friend and award-winning community entrepreneur) and I organised thousands of council tenants and stopped the sale of their houses to property developers at prices well below market value. As a by-product, we won funding for several neighbourhood advice centres in the poorest estates – and for a city-wide law centre in Gloucester, in the UK. These new projects represented people and secured their benefits and entitlements. We used the law to bring about social change. What I didn't know was that by doing this we were helping to open the door to 'no win, no fee'.

*'Whether we are safe and secure in our neighbourhoods is largely within our domain. Many studies show there are two major determinants of our local safety. One is how many neighbours we know by name. The second is how often we are present and associated in public - outside our houses.'* **John McKnight**[39]

No longer are accidents just accidents, but opportunities to level blame and look for financial compensation. Individuals are encouraged to exaggerate their physical and emotional pain, to appear weak and traumatised. This makes everyone ever more cautious and less likely to take on any responsibility for informal social activities outside their home or workplace.

Doctors, teachers and other local authority workers are put on the defensive and might limit their activities in order to avoid risk. The final irony is that compensation payments are often paid with public money taken from budgets meant to pay for over-stretched and under-financed public services. We are the losers yet again.

## Safety in numbers

By taking small, calculated risks and participating in community life people can do more to protect themselves than by doing anything else. By being connected with others, by learning more about what is going on in their local area, and by having a social identity, people build a really effective social-support system that protects everyone. The impression that our communities are no longer safe places to work and live is completely false, but they may become so if we depopulate them and disconnect from each other.

*'Hope remains only in the most difficult task of all: to reconsider everything from the ground up, so as to shape a living society inside a dying society.'* **Albert Camus**, Existentialist[40]

## Women's work

Women were once the engines of the core economy, the ones who reached out to a lonely neighbour, brought people together in difficult times and rallied round in emergencies. Their resilience, adaptability and pragmatism came up with innovative local solutions to social problems time and time again. They nurtured the children, cared for the sick and elderly, and were around in day-time to sustain neighbourliness and the core economy. This once traditionally female role now needs to be extended to everyone; women will be the first to suffer in any economic recession and we all need to take more responsibility for preserving the core economy. People need to draw a line, to take a stand and rebuild our core economy now!

Studies by Volunteering England and the NCVO have repeatedly shown that whenever people volunteer and participate more fully in community life, they increase their interpersonal skills, they understand other people better, and they learn how to motivate others and to deal with difficult situations.

Malte Klar and Tim Kasser, social scientists, were widely reported in the press when they announced that their studies had shown that activists are happier and more optimistic people. They said that taking action over social issues makes us feel better, more purposeful and more alive. Creature comforts and relative affluence just do not compare. Social activists are 'more enriched than those who merely complain' and came out strongest on all of the vitality scales.

Funmi Olowe, the time-broker at the Clapham Park Time Bank in South London, told me that nothing else unified and motivated her members as much as when they persuaded the authorities to change a decision.

Time and again, hour by hour, we have seen people at time banks become happier and more fulfilled simply through connecting more to the people who live around them.

Archbishop Desmond Tutu speaks often about the essence of being human. He claims that you can't exist as a human being in isolation and when you have 'Ubuntu' you are known for your generosity. We think of ourselves far too frequently as just individuals, separated from one another, whereas we are connected. When you do well, it spreads out. Taking him at his word some friends and I have agreed to meet for 'Togetherness Walks' every few weeks. When like minds and open hearts come together it can be transformative – and an excellent way to make social use of social space in public parks. There's room for more – so join us.

What have you got to lose?
You might have a lot to gain…
And so might we…
Make contact with us via Andy at **www.frameworks4change.co.uk**

*'The human experience is finite - it will end - surely we should all be pulling together to make everyone's experience a happy one? Timebanking not only directly helps people meet each other and make new friendships and relationships, it tells us more about ourselves and our potential.'* **Saskia**, London

# Chapter 4
# We are all in this together: public space

*'Communities had to be created, fought for, tended like gardens. They expanded or contracted with the dreams of men.'* **Barack Obama**

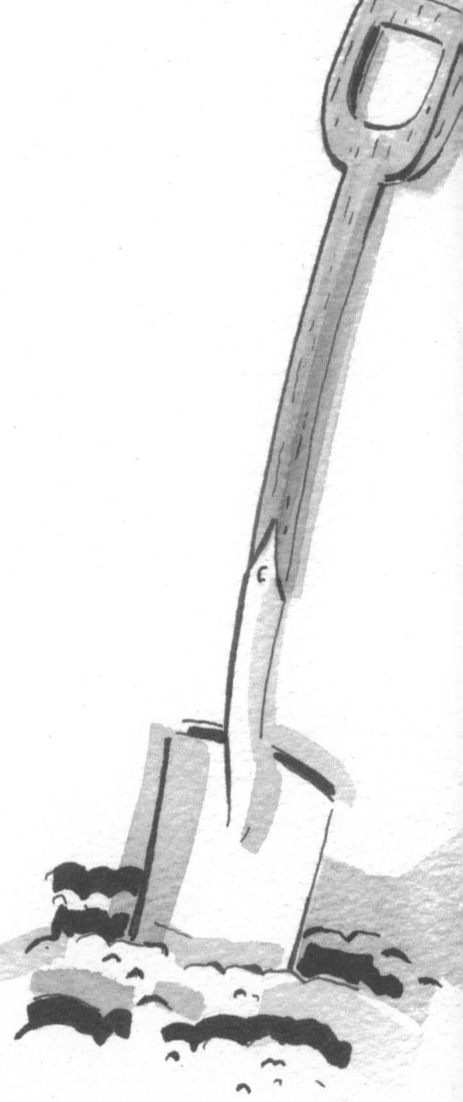

**FOR SEVERAL YEARS, right up until I had kids of my own, I ran a therapeutic community for troubled young people in the Black Mountains in Wales. Small groups of young offenders aged between 14 and 18, and from the inner cities, would come and live at the centre as a community. Their social workers, probation officers and teachers were with them and, in time, they all formed an attachment to the staff and to the centre. It became a safe place for the young people to question their previous anti-social and self-destructive behaviours.**

We had access to mountains, rivers and caves, but the biggest asset that we had was the young people themselves. They were intelligent, perceptive, energetic, quick-witted and often great fun to have around. They drew up the activity programmes at the start of each week and agreed a set of rules for living together. (The severity of punishments and penalties for breaking these rules that were suggested by the young people did sometimes need softening!) While at the centre, the young people and their carers began to treat each other more as equals – mutual trust has to grow quickly when you are at either end of a rope on a 30-metre abseil.

In the evenings, we ran group-therapy sessions and almost without exception the adults would apologise at some point for the way they had been relating to the young people, for the professional personas that they had felt they had to adopt. It was difficult to keep these more open relationships going when they went back to the city, but while they were on the 18-month programme, no-one re-offended. My hope is that we planted enough seeds of care and trust so that when the young people had children of their own they would break the negative cycle in which their own families seemed trapped.

The two lessons I took with me from this rewarding work experience, just as relevant today, for anyone running a public or voluntary service were to always:

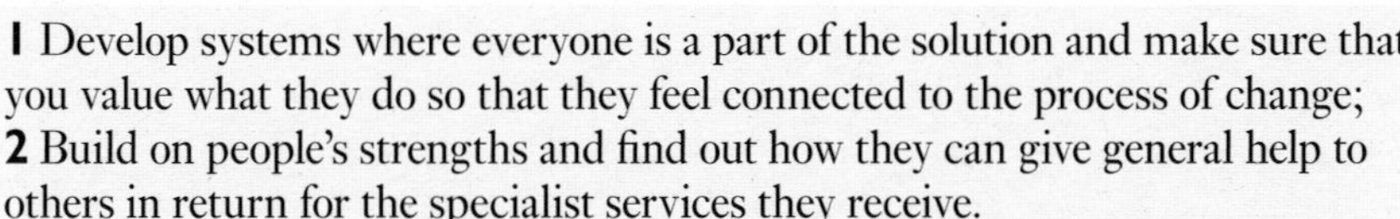

**1** Develop systems where everyone is a part of the solution and make sure that you value what they do so that they feel connected to the process of change; **2** Build on people's strengths and find out how they can give general help to others in return for the specialist services they receive.

Many years later I discovered that at the very same time that I was running the centre in Wales, the Nobel Prize-winning economist, Elinor Ostrom, was coming to the same conclusions I had, and was formulating the concept of 'co-production'. She noted that when the police lost their informal connections with local communities and switched from walking the streets to working in offices and in cars they no longer received nor seemed to value the knowledge and intelligence that local people had supplied them with in the past. As a result their criminal detection rates plummeted.

For the very latest thinking on co-production see 'Co-Production 2.0: Retrofitting Human Service Programs to Tap the Renewable Energy of Community' by Edgar Cahn. Available at **www.timebanking.org**.

Co-production theory has now become a widely accepted approach and Timebanking is recognised as an ideal tool to deliver it. If our public services do not ask for and value contributions from those they are trying to help – their 'service users', their families, friends, neighbours and the wider community – then local people are unlikely to feel connected and, worse still, will get the impression that they have nothing to offer. Health, wellbeing, education, community cohesion, caring citizenship – you name it – cannot be delivered by professional strangers. Like community organisers, public-service workers need to ask people what they need, find the common ground, and find ways to move forward together. The message that needs to go out to individuals and communities is: *'We can do it together, but we cannot do it without you.'* Unfortunately, the message that too often goes out, albeit unconsciously, is: *'We are here to help you but you have little that we value or need.'*

This is a poem written by an old woman who was in a geriatric ward in a London hospital. The poem was found in her locker after her death. The nurses thought she could neither read nor write. Many thanks to Trevor T. Smith, actor and playwright, for recovering it.

*'Let's usher in a new era of mutual volunteering on a very small scale - but in a wide variety of communities - but then, as they used to say in the first time bank in Miami: small plus small plus small equals large.'* **David Boyle**[41]

**WHAT DO YOU SEE**, nurses, what do you see?
Are you thinking when you are looking at me –
A crabbit old woman, not very wise,
Uncertain of habit with faraway eyes,
Who dribbles her food and makes no reply,
When you say in a loud voice, 'I do wish you'd try'
I'll tell you who I am, as I sit here so still,
As I rise at your bidding, as I eat at your will.
I'm a child of ten with a father and mother,
With brothers and sisters who love one another,
A bride soon at twenty, my heart gives a leap
Remembering the vows I promised to keep:
At twenty-five now I have young of my own,
Who need me to build a secure happy home.
At fifty once more babies play round my knee,
Again we know children, my loved one and me.
Dark days upon me, my husband is dead,
I look at the future, I shudder with dread.
My young are all busy rearing young of their own
And I think of the years and the love I have known.
I'm an old woman now and nature is cruel,
'Tis her jest to make old age look like a fool,
The body it crumbles, grace and vigour depart,
There is now a stone where once was a heart,
But inside this old carcass a young girl still dwells
And now and again my battered heart swells.
I remember the joys, I remember the pains,
And I'm loving the living all over again,
And I think of the years all too few – gone too fast
And accept the stark fact that nothing will last.
So open your eyes, nurses, open and see
Not a crabbit old woman, look close – and see me.

Baroness Julia Neuberger recently headed up the Commission on the Future of Volunteering, which concluded that we need to 'put mutuality back into the DNA of society'. Her thinking was informed by her personal experiences in various hospitals, as she cared for a relation who was dying. The treatment they received was all but inhuman, until they went to a place where volunteers played a large part. This hospice welcomed volunteers (much like hospitals 30 years ago), and they transformed the atmosphere. They had time to care, to listen and to empathise; the patients benefitted enormously – and so did the staff.

In Lehigh Hospital in Philadelphia, patients returning home after treatment are asked if they want help settling back into a routine at home. Shopping, cleaning, running errands, looking after pets, etc., are provided free by volunteers. The patients only have to agree to volunteer for others in the future when they are feeling better. The hospital has a regular supply of over 500 volunteers, all keen to pay back and make a difference.

Health and social-care policy in this country is now committed to 'personalisation and prevention' (and early intervention). At the same time, their services are facing massive cutbacks and they will continue to face them for the foreseeable future. They may not all not know it yet, but Timebanking is one of the ways they will be able to provide 'more for less' and improve the quality of their services.

People were once connected to the places where they lived and valued their local reputations as good neighbours, active citizens and supporters of civic life. Local people knew what skills others had, and who was likely to respond positively when called upon for help. People trusted each other and traded favours in the knowledge that if they did so, others would be more likely to be there for them when they needed it. This is how 'social capital' was created, and provided platforms for self-sustaining, cohesive and capable communities.

Timebanking is helping to reverse the current scaling-down of social capital and is creating new types of social networks that make it easy for peo-

*'Investment in social capital is not an alternative to, but is a prerequisite for, political mobilisation and reform.'* **Robert D. Putnam**, Professor of Public Policy at Harvard[42]

ple to come together to share their skills, reflect on issues of common concern, and take action to improve things for each other and for the wider community. Time banks are already offering practical, effective, affordable, socially beneficial and sustainable ways to support citizens to generate their own solutions through mutual aid. The work of many professionals is now quite rightly aimed at preventing social problems before they cost too much to put right. They try to make sure that the services provided are led by the needs of the service user, so that the service user can be more in control of their own lives.

They try to 'shape' the places where people live, so that they may be happier, safer and more prosperous. In future, this will mean that professionals will spend less time managing services and overseeing budgets, and more time supporting communities and searching out opportunities and incentives for local people to become involved as active citizens and good neighbours.

Therefore, their immediate priority needs to be the creation of new, safe, local social networks, where people can learn together about their rights and their responsibilities as citizens. Timebanking is the ideal tool for them to achieve these objectives.

## Timebanking in the community

In Newsome, Yorkshire, Timebanking has helped the community to protect its Grade II-listed mill (threatened by theft, vandalism, arson and neglect) by sharing information, engaging people in the planning process and bringing people together. Timebankers ran a door-to-door survey as part of the ongoing campaign to retain Newsome Mill Ponds and the former mill-workers' allotments. The resulting research report demonstrated the huge demand for local allotments, helping to win an eleventh-hour planning appeal. This work also gave rise to the 'Growing Newsome' project, through which timebankers are supporting each other and the wider community in growing their own local food.

This mirrors the plans that policy-makers have for our public services, putting people, rather than systems and procedures, first.

Public services will need to take more time to:

■ **Ask local people what they want.** Inviting people to respond to agendas that are based on achieving national targets set by professional strangers is quite pointless. By contrast, the continual gathering of information and opinions on social issues, collating them, prioritising them, helping people to act on them and reporting back to people on any progress is what is required for any significant levels of community engagement. It is unlikely that resources will ever be found to pay for this but time banks can pay people in time credits for this invaluable work. When they do, local people soon become welcomed advocates and facilitators. They operate street-by-street and everyone feels valued as a source of intelligence – and believe that they are being listened to and appreciated. Everyone feels connected and so more inclined to contribute their time and energy to solving social problems. The 'street ambassadors' scheme run by Dawn Davies and her team at the Timecentre in Blaengarw, South Wales is a fine example of this process in action (see page 90 for more about the Timecentre).

■ **Offer incentives for people to get involved.** Expecting people to give time and energy to tackle social problems for the sake of a 'community spirit', which may have disappeared years ago, is completely unrealistic. Setting aside ten percent of any budget allocated for a community initiative to say 'thank you' to people when they get involved will, by contrast, raise the levels of involvement dramatically. By showing that they value people's skills and energy by rewarding them with access to cultural events, free places on training courses, use of leisure facilities and organised outings to places of interest, public services and voluntary agencies can cement the bonds between them and the community. The agency can record the hours of involvement and issue time credits that entitle people to a menu of rewards that have been jointly chosen. Most time banks have a whole range of ways of saying thank you and they often receive donations of free and discounted services, preferential booking rights and complimentary admissions to events from local councils and from national and local businesses. (The King's Cross Time Bank in London, run by Sam Hopley and his team at the Holy Cross Centre, is an excellent example. They work closely with the local authority and provide a range of incentives sponsored by local businesses.)

## Catalysts for change

Local authorities will certainly need to be friendlier and more open places so that people feel comfortable enough to come forward to share in designing and delivering these new ideas and practices like co-production and Timebanking. Public forums are required for people to meet and speak their minds, to reflect together on what needs to be done, and on how best to get organised and co-create long-term solutions. In exchange for supporting time banks, local authorities can bank on the co-operation, knowledge and skills of members of the community on an unprecedented scale.

Over the past ten years, many local authorities, health- and social-care providers, voluntary organisations and local communities have set up time banks to provide the neutral space, incentives and relationships needed to achieve three key goals, as identified in the New Economics Foundation's report by Josh Ryan-Collins, 'A Wealth of Time':[43]

- Making people more powerful;
- Preventing needs arising; and
- Engaging sustainable resources.

Community organisations, self-help groups, the police, probation, prisons, hospitals, schools, youth clubs, churches, housing organisations and environmental groups have been experimenting with Timebanking and changing how they work with, and relate to, their service users, their families and the wider community.

'All staff get the chance to volunteer in the community for two days a week each year, but it is now done through the time bank. Staff can keep the time credits they earn for community work or donate them back to the Primary Care Trust, who then pay them to local people to encourage them to attend courses and join in activities that mean that they are living more healthy lives.' **Dan**, Sandwell

## Relationships, relationships, relationships

*'There are good reasons for putting relationships at the core of effective public provision. Relationships are at the heart of what makes for a good life. Living as a solitary individual, for most people, is a recipe for unhappiness. Much of what we most value – love, friendship, trust, recognition, care – comes from relationships with family, friends and social networks. People grow up well and age well if they have supportive relationships … for most of the last decade, we have seen public services as systems and standards, to be managed and rationalised … Instead, we should re-imagine public services as feeding the relationships that sustain us in everyday life … Target-setting destroys the empathetic engaging and creative aspects that make us human – undermines people, diminishes confidence in themselves, and capacity to solve problems – it kills convivial relationships.'* **Charlie Leadbeater**, Writer[44]

Relationships are essential for building social capital and can also be used as the basis for solving the most serious of our social ills. Circles of Support and Accountability, run by the Quakers and others, are a good example. They work with high-risk sexual offenders on their release from prison. They aim to reduce victimisation and to help integration back into society. Four to six local volunteers receive training and form a 'circle' around the offender and offer practical, physical and emotional support. The offender agrees to stop offending and to take advice on living a productive life. The circle helps him stick to his promise. Such straightforward, inexpensive interventions have reduced re-offending by 83 percent. Rather than being obliged to live outside society, the offender is given the chance to belong to a community that is honouring its collective responsibilities to those who live there.

So often, however, public services fail to invest in simple, straightforward solutions; and, even when they do, they inadvertently place artificial limits on their potency, mainly around accountability for the money involved and by undervaluing their greatest asset – the local community.

## The parable of the squares and the blobs

A group of philanthropists wondered why it was that when they selected a social issue and gave money to help the proposed solutions things only seemed to get worse. To try to understand better what was happening, they labelled the organisations they funded 'squares' (public service agencies and voluntary groups were examples of squares), and they labelled the people in the community who clustered informally in groups, 'blobs'. The blobs, everyone agreed at the outset, had the energy, the vitality, the contacts, the knowledge, many of the skills and the social networks that were needed to deal with the problems; but, the philanthropist's money stayed with the squares because they knew how to manage and account for it.

However much the squares promised to reach out in the community and get to the root causes of the issue they never seemed to get there. Some sort of a gulf separated the squares from the blobs. The philanthropists tried to bridge the gulf by funding partnerships between the squares and the blobs - but the squares still kept most of the money. They tried next to give some of the money directly to the blobs. Then something strange happened; the blobs were asked to turn themselves into little squares so that they could be trusted to look after their part of the money. By the time all the training, meetings and reports were done, the blobs had ceased to be blobs.[45]

As discussed in Chapter 1, market-led solutions are not always appropriate. Employing a community-based person can feel like progress, but often the worker inhabits a no-man's-land in between the agency and the community. The option now open to agencies is to invest those same resources in mobilising the skills and energies of local people to deliver community solutions through the semi-formal framework of a time bank.

A time bank provides a security blanket or safety net for current service users that can break the cycle of dependency and help people to try out new relationships and opportunities. They can help others in return for the services they receive from professionals and specialists, grow in self-esteem and confidence, and become valued members of a local community.

Anne was referred to her local time bank by the Post-Traumatic Stress Disorder Clinic at the Maudsley Hospital. Aran, her 15-year-old son, lived alone at home with his mother.

Funmi and Ros, the time-brokers, welcomed Anne as a participant and looked for her strengths. She quickly earned over 100 time credits by doing gardening for other members of the time bank, and in a local community garden. She found gardening, a new experience for her, immensely enjoyable, fulfilling and a chance to relax – and it dramatically reduced her number of hospital re-admissions. Unfortunately, Aran was getting deeper into trouble with the police and had been excluded from school. He was on a court order, and the magistrate had made it clear that this was absolutely his last chance of avoiding custody.

Anne asked her community for help through the time bank. She could do this as an equal, not as a victim. She used her time credits to 'buy in' the help she needed – as any responsible parent would. She felt Aran urgently needed a positive role model, and the time bank found a guy, slightly older, but from the same culture and background, to become his friend and mentor.

The mentor earned time credits for being there at the end of a phone when he was needed, and for spending an hour or more with Aran each week.

This relationship provided the breakthrough that was hoped for and Aran agreed to stay out of trouble and attend the Young People in Crisis Project.

As a payback, a local gym and an ice-skating rink let Aran pay for sessions in time credits rather than in cash (which he didn't have). Aran earned his time credits by helping out in the community and holding to his promise not to go out with his old mates, to be back in his house by 9pm every evening, and to ring his mentor regularly. Other time-bank members called by the house to check he was in.

These new friendship links with other adults meant that when Anne had a relapse and had to go into the acute ward for a few days – and on another occasion when she needed a week's respite care – Aran was happy for two of them to move into his house, care for him, and help to keep him out of trouble while his mother was away.

Members of his new time-bank extended family also kept in contact with the various social-care agencies to make sure Aran was not forgotten, and that specialist skills were still available to help and support him. Some

## Staying well

Keeping people safe, well and fit for work is not generally undertaken by professionals. They only come into action when people are in trouble or ill.

In South London, however, the Rushey Green Health Centre has operated a time bank for nine years. It was set up by Shelley McKowen and is now run by Philippe Granger and Charmaine Jacobs. Doctors write prescriptions for medication but also for group activities, a regular hourly visit from a local time-bank participant, help with shopping, or a friendly voice over the telephone from someone who has been through the same surgery facing a worried patient. All of the time-bank participants are patients of the surgery, and are happy to co-produce the care and support they all need to stay well; they earn their time credits at the same time. The doctors report that time-bank participants come to their surgeries less often, and that the time bank frees up time for them to give more to their patients needing medical treatment.

Further, Timebanking has shown that people are much more likely to keep well if they pair up informally with neighbours, friends or family, with other time-bank members, and keep each other motivated through mutual encouragement and shared goals.

*'If, in the past decade, the NHS has come to understand that health services are measurably improved by the patient's voice, in the next 20 we will come to understand that they can only be delivered with the citizen's hand.'* **Dr Paul Hodgkin**, Sheffield

of Aran's old friends saw what was going on and joined the time bank. They too have contributed to the wellbeing of their local community; in fact, one of them has earned over 600 time credits.

Anne has been out of hospital now for two years. Aran is attending college and has continued to stay out of trouble.

Timebanking provides a safe way for public services to reach out to the community. There are safeguards built into the system and a national umbrella organisation to maintain standards. Timebanking UK has introduced a Kitemark for local authority-run time banks to ensure that people are safe and have a meaningful and positive experience. Full details are available on their website: **www.timebanking.org**.

Doctors can prescribe the right drugs, but are powerless to provide what they know is by far the best medication – friends, family, social networks and something useful to do. We all urgently need to place a higher value on the everyday circles of mutual support that have been a part of the social environment for generations and were the bedrock of the welfare state and of the NHS. We also need to take on responsibility for our own wellbeing (see opposite).

## Five ways to wellbeing: The evidence

**CONNECT:** With the people around you. With family, friends, colleagues and neighbours. At home, work, school or in your local community. Think of these as the cornerstones of your life and invest time in developing them. Building these connections will support and enrich you every day.

**BE ACTIVE:** Go for a walk or run. Step outside. Cycle. Play a game. Garden. Dance. Exercising makes you feel good. Most importantly, discover a physical activity you enjoy and that suits your level of mobility and fitness.

**TAKE NOTICE:** Be curious. Catch sight of the beautiful. Remark on the unusual. Notice the changing seasons. Savour the moment, whether you are walking to work, eating lunch or talking to friends. Be aware of the world around you and what you are feeling. Reflecting on your experiences will help you appreciate what matters to you.

**KEEP LEARNING:** Try something new. Rediscover an old interest. Sign up for that course. Take on a different responsibility at work. Fix a bike. Learn to play an instrument or how to cook your favourite food. Set a challenge you enjoy achieving. Learning new things will make you more confident as well as being fun.

**GIVE:** Do something nice for a friend, or a stranger. Thank someone. Smile. Volunteer your time. Join a community group. Look out, as well as in. Seeing yourself and your happiness as linked to the wider community can be incredibly rewarding, and creates connections with the people around you.

*Published by the New Economics Foundation*[46]

# A complete culture change for our public services

If you are involved in delivering services that aim to improve people's resilience, opportunities and wellbeing – be it an institution, a front-line agency, a voluntary or community organisation or a self-help group – you need to ask yourself some fundamental questions: Do your systems and procedures assist the formation of interdependent relationships among those you are now helping? Or, are you, all be it inadvertently, making people dependent on your specialist skills? The following seven questions are well worth reflecting upon:

**1** Do you ask your members, users, clients, pupils or participants what they enjoy doing for others?

**2** Do you look out for regular opportunities for them to help others?

**3** Do you welcome their involvement in the running of your organisation, and do you log the time that they work for you?

**4** Do you reward them for their co-operation?

**5** Do you ask them to pay back for the specialist services they receive from you by giving more general help to others?

**6** Do you organise opportunities for mutual support between peers, either one-to-one or in groups?

**7** Do you participate in local events and community activities alongside your service users and their families, friends and neighbours?

Timebanking is a tool for you to use at very little financial cost to help you to sustain a social environment where everyone can become a valued contributor to their own and to other people's wellbeing and happiness.

This chapter has been about public space and so to complete our analogy with public parks I know of no finer example of a direct collaboration between local services and local people in a public space than Townstal Play Park in Devon. A drab cement area in an isolated and disadvantaged area has been transformed into a stimulating, fun and colourful play area. This new treasured community asset was designed by the children, with a sympathetic architect, and the money was raised by local people and the council together.

*'So how, as a society, can we influence whether people are happy? We are inherently social, and our happiness depends above all on the quality of our relationships with other people. We have to develop public policies that take this relationship factor into account.'* **Richard Layard**, Economist and Author[47]

# Chapter 5
# A social climate change: Timebanking

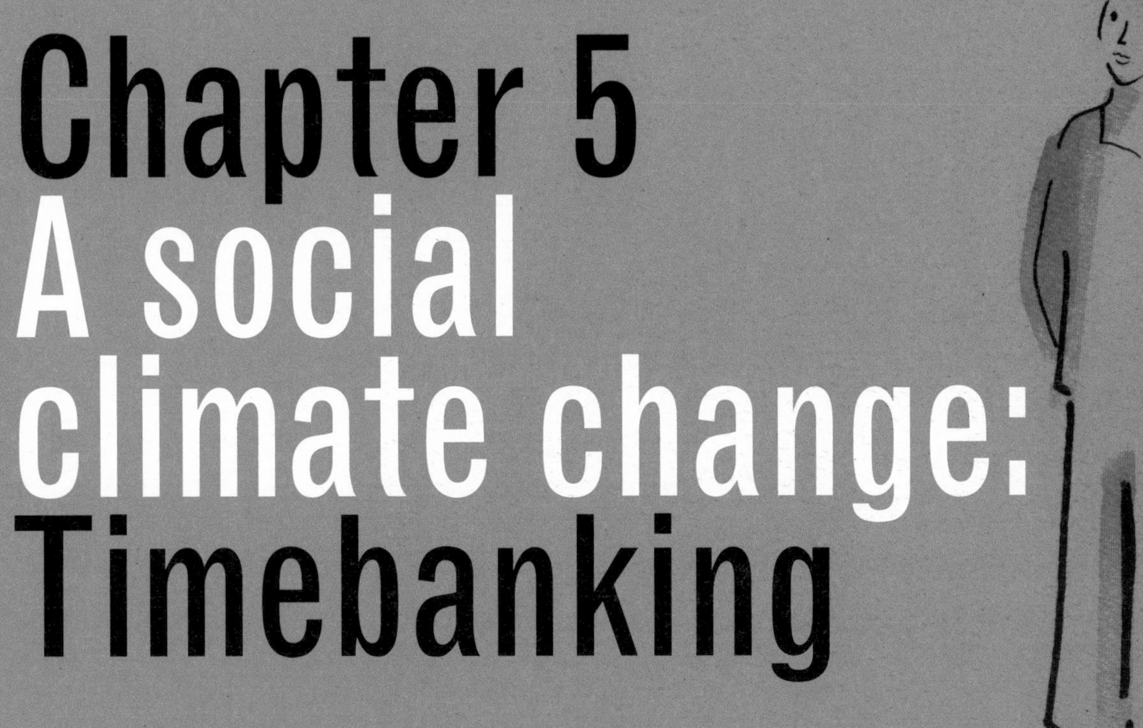

*'If you want to build a ship, don't drum up the men to gather*

**THE EXCHANGE OF 'GIFTS', 'favours' and 'stories' has always taken place in and between communities. These exchanges mean far more than the actual items, tasks or information involved. They are reminders of a common history, of the acts of reciprocity that have passed between their communities in the past. They also send powerful messages about the status of the relationship in the present.**

In Britain today, when a gift is given it is still expected that the person receiving the gift will at some point in the future give a gift back in return. The decision about the value and timing of any gift to be given in return is often left open. Over and above the actual receipt of the gifts, people therefore share in an exchange of trust, respect and mutual self-esteem. Further, the appreciation and approval they each receive for the thought and care they have put into choosing their gift becomes a strong incentive to carry on exchanging gifts.

Extended families work in the same way. There is an expectation that in return for what you do for other family members, you will receive the same care and attention you need in return. This is based partly on trust (sometimes guilt), on an intimate knowledge of the other members of the family, and, above all, on a sense of family loyalty. This all makes it very unlikely that your relations will deny their moral obligations to you in the future.

This gift exchange was once the norm in most communities and it was the way that most social care was delivered. However, social care is fast becoming a commercial enterprise with one-way delivery systems – from a paid professional or volunteer to a passive receiver. This has meant that a 'gift exchange' of care in communities is not developing as it once did. This natural system for caring for each other is further threatened by an increasingly mobile and work-orientated society. People no longer know their neighbours or what they need, and seem to want – above all else – to protect their privacy. The Happy Planet Index[48] rated relative happiness levels in 22 countries and found that in the UK people were the least likely of all the countries studied to know neighbours, were the least connected, and had the worst family relationships in Europe.

*wood, divide the work and give orders. Instead, teach them to yearn for the vast and endless sea.'* **Antoine de Saint-Exupery**

## A new way to do it

Timebanking offers a modern, safe, powerful way to bring back the mutual (gift) exchange of skills, favours and stories, and is now widely recognised as a potent antidote to our drift toward isolation.

Rather than beads or blips on a screen, Timebanking uses 'time' as a medium of exchange. A fixed value is given to an hour of care, encouragement, training, practical and emotional support, or kindness by marking every hour with a new currency called time credits. One hour earns the giver one time credit and the receiver pays the time bank – the local community – one time credit. The exchange is recorded electronically at the time bank and shows up as a debit or a credit in each person's time bank account. The giver knows that in return he or she will receive an hour's help when needed, and can use the time credits to 'purchase' skills from other members of the community.

He or she also receives respect and appreciation from the receiver and from a new extended local 'family'. The receiver is an equally important contributor to the time-bank system because by asking for the help he or she needs, others are given the opportunity to be useful and to earn time credits. The asking is made so much easier by knowing that there will be an opportunity to pay back and earn time credits by providing a skill or a service to someone else at some point in the future.

The more people ask, the more the currency circulates and the more everyone benefits. Just like the more traditional 'gift exchange', the time-bank system makes sure that every 'gift' is matched by another act of kindness or practical support. Just as in an extended family or a thriving community, there are no contracts or cash involved; the obligation to reciprocate is just a moral one. It is the unexpected encounters, the stories, the skills people share, as well as the time credits they earn, that people report motivates them to keep on Timebanking.

*'The new money circulating from the time bank functions a little like the pat on the back that people used to get in stable neighbourhood settings, where good deeds became part of a collective memory that would one day return in the form of kindness to themselves.'* **Edgar Cahn** and **Jonathan Rowe**[49]

*'Whereas money comes from on high and is passed around anonymously, time credits are created at the grass roots by two parties who have both their names on them. If we value volunteer hours, we value the volunteers, we value people. There is no shortage of this currency. Anybody can create it by working an hour. Volunteer work, by definition, is not done for reward. The volunteer instead gets credit. This credit build-up represents the value of the volunteer in the community. Volunteer credits make people the source and repository of value. The credits accumulate human capital.'* **Derek Brownlee**, Author[50]

With Timebanking, everyone can afford the support they need just by being prepared to do what they can to help out others in return.

The first Timebanking story I heard was about Ana Miyares, a corporate banker turned Timebanking pioneer. She had built a time bank in Florida, with over 3,000 members. Among them were many Cuban immigrants, two of whom were suffering from 'spousal abuse'. These women were classic victims – being treated violently, living in a culture that was alien to them, and unable to speak the language. They worried that if they complained about their situation, they might get into more trouble. If these women were lucky, a typical benevolent response might have been a law firm representing them on a pro bono basis. Their husbands would have been served with injunctions and the women would have been passive receivers of a specialist service from professional strangers.

Timebanking turned the situation on its head. A law firm agreed to represent the women, but asked for time dollars (time credits in the USA) in return. Every hour of legal work was to be matched with an hour of voluntary community work. The women went out into their community and earned a time dollar for every hour that they spent sharing what they learned about the legal process, spousal abuse and the immigration policy. They were trusted and could communicate with other women who were in similar predicaments. Their work did not go unnoticed in the wider community and they were soon invited to present a weekly local radio advice programme for Cuban immigrants. They had transformed themselves into local role models and it was all made possible by some enlightened professionals and a new 'social money' called time dollars. I was intrigued.

My Timebanking education continued when I met Diana McCourt. At this time, she was running Womanshare, one of the first time banks in the USA, and was, according to the New York Times, 'leading a social revolution'. Her time bank was providing women with new friendships, and a valuable system for self-help and encouragement 'to live life more joyfully'.

In his book, Funny Money[51], author and new economist, David Boyle,

*'Community currency allows localities and regions to create needs with the under-utilised resources. It also provides a way rather than being siphoned off to distant companies.'*

quotes Diana: *'We're discovering that doing tasks together has a beauty and power that goes far beyond the work. We're also finding that some shares are just about being in the presence of another – having the comfort of another person on hand when you have an onerous task to do.'*

I remember looking at the extensive lists of skills that were on offer from the members – things like yoga, carpentry, cooking, sewing, knitting, quilting, dancing lessons, decorating, decision-making, home repairs, jewellery-making, fitness training, poetry reading, use of power tools, dealing with the menopause, desktop publishing, T'ai chi, massage, self-marketing, self-expression, and on, and on …

It was then that I understood that every community has an equally impressive array of local talent that is being discounted simply because it is potentially in plentiful supply. Market thinking is blinding us to the simple truth that ordinary everyday skills are a priceless resource that can bring real value to the process of rebuilding our communities.

I was struck also by the flexibility of the Timebanking system. People can dip in and out as they wish, as there will be times in every life when we need that extra bit of help and other times when we have spare time to give.

## The 'United' Kingdom

In October 1998, Joy Robinson and I set up the first time bank in the UK, in Stonehouse, a small town in Gloucestershire. We called it 'Fair Shares', and it now operates across the county with over 850 members, who exchange over 50,000 time credits each year. That first time bank, like the hundreds that have followed, matched unused resources with unmet needs. The local area was made up of older people and young single parents and their children. The older people had a lifetime of parenting skills and the young parents were fit and mobile. It didn't take an Einstein to see all the practical ways that they could be of use to each other. All they needed was to be reconnected to each

*real wealth in their local economy by matching the unmet for the wealth that is produced locally to benefit local people,*

**Bernard Lietaer** and **Gwendolyn Hallsmith**, Social Entrepreneurs[52]

other and reintroduced to the basic building blocks of community life – give and take. They did the rest themselves and the time bank is still flourishing today. It has never had to pay an outsider to 'manage' the project; people earn time credits for running the time bank as well as for helping one another out.

The model to which we introduced them was simple:

- An hour of involvement is rewarded with one 'time credit', a community loyalty point.
- Time credits are deposited at the time bank and can then be spent when needed on services from other local people.
- A software programme holds a local information system on who is available, when and with what skills.
- The time bank provides a safe, broad-based framework for connecting people and acts as a letter of introduction.
- Once in circulation, the 'time-based local currency' takes on a meaning of its own and is every bit as real as the cash in people's pockets.

This has remained the essence of Timebanking in the UK ever since and, over the past ten years, the Timebanking system has been refined and is now 'well fit' for purpose.

In their Community Currency Guide, Bernard Lietaer and Gwendolyn Hallsmith compare the various models of new business practice with those of the complementary currency movement and their work has helped many people to overcome their doubts about the potential power and viability of community currencies generally.

An easily understood example is the development of 'frequent-flyer miles'. They were originally no more that a marketing gimmick for the few airlines who issued them, and they could only be used to buy tickets on their flights. Now 14 trillion airline miles have been issued by five global airline alliances, which is more than all the dollars and euro bills in circulation combined.

What's more, their field of operations has expanded and they can be earned just by using a credit card, and they are redeemable for booklets full

of products. For example, it is now estimated that only one-third of British Airways' air miles are used to buy airline tickets. In a very short space of time, air miles have become a significant 'complementary currency', albeit with a specific commercial objective – customer loyalty. An unused resource, empty airline seats, has been used to meet an unmet need; the consumers search for a bargain, and at the same time the name of the airline has been associated in people's minds with fair play.

What we are doing by Timebanking is exactly the same and we hope to become as acceptable and even more valuable to the general public – as our purpose is to strengthen the social environment, not just make profits for our shareholders.

We have begun in a small way by utilising unused resources, including tickets for cinema seats, leisure-centre facilities, training places and social and cultural events – and by no means least, all of the unused talents and skills and energy of local people – to mobilise neighbourhood loyalty and to meet all the unmet needs of the wider community. As stated, there is no good reason why Timebanking does not become every bit as powerful a community currency as frequent-flyer miles and we have the added advantage of a currency that is created by the actions of individuals in communities. Unlike air miles, we can avoid overreaching ourselves and making promises we cannot fulfil.

Just as in the business world, three models of exchange have emerged in time banks; however, they are interdependent and interconnected. A fully developed time bank incorporates all three models.

## Model one: person-to-person

The 'person-to-person' model of Timebanking is where people use time credits as the medium of exchange as if it were conventional money, but without any pricing system; one hour is always one time credit. It is called a 'mutual credit system' by community-currency theorists and is the one reflected in

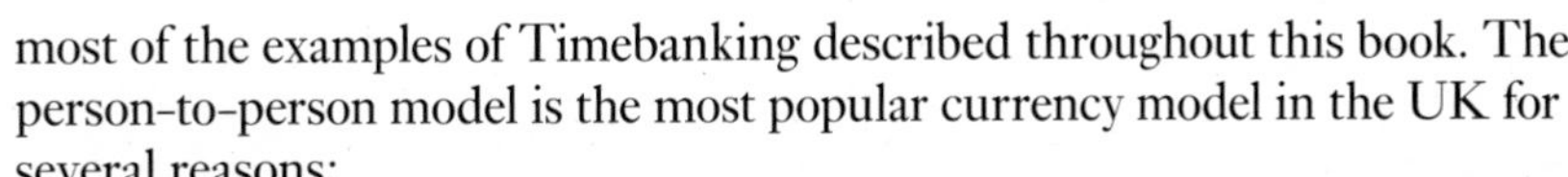

most of the examples of Timebanking described throughout this book. The person-to-person model is the most popular currency model in the UK for several reasons:

- people do not have to pay any interest so they can borrow from the system and can pay back whenever they want;
- people actually create the time credits necessary for the transactions themselves by simply agreeing to exchange their skills;
- the system self-regulates and always has sufficient currency available;
- there is no risk of inflation – the social money that is created, by definition, always perfectly matches its need.

## Model two: agency-to-person

Currencies, like frequent-flyer miles, discount vouchers and store cards are known as 'loyalty currencies' because their purpose is to encourage the customer to return. This is similar to the 'agency-to-person' model of Timebanking, which is called a 'fiat credit system' by the theorists.

In this model, the time credits are distributed by a host organisation both to encourage people to behave in a certain way and to improve the image of the organisation itself. The time credits are given to people in exchange for their participation, and can be cashed in for a menu of rewards. In this model, the time credits sometimes take the form of an actual paper currency. This can be an advantage, as the model is easier to manage because people exchange the paper currency themselves so there is no need to record every transaction on the computer. It also has its drawbacks because, as they learned in Argentina, paper currencies can be counterfeited. They can also be 'traded' outside the system by the more 'entrepreneurial' members.

This model was developed in South Wales by Geoff Thomas and his team, and has been extremely successful. Local authorities and voluntary agencies are testing the model for the provision of low-level social care, environmental work, turning young people into active citizens, in schools and for building community among tenants of housing organisations. As Geoff says, the mistake has been to airbrush mutuality out of our public services. The agency-to-person model is beginning the long process of rectifying this by giving people incentives to become active again as citizens and encouraging paid staff to become facilitators rather than providers.

The success of one particular community centre that has transformed itself into a thriving 'time centre' by using this model has caused a great deal of interest. The Blaengarw Timecentre is in a small town at the top of the Garw Valley in Wales. The coal pits have long gone and there is a high level of unemployment, but there is a relatively stable population. The Timecentre is run by the Creation Development Trust and is now a much-loved and well-used arts and community venue. But its 250-seat auditorium, with a stage, licensed bar, childcare room, dance studio, IT suite, offices and activity rooms, were once unused. The building's assets are now providing catalysts to build new social networks and improve individual wellbeing; they are bringing the community back to life.

Local people earn one time credit for each hour they give to the running of the centre or to the community, and spend the time credits on using the equipment and facilities at the Timecentre – or for social and educational events, trips and community activities. To attend events at the centre, people can pay with time credits, hour for hour, whether it's bingo, opera, choirs, comedy nights or a party. For example, a three-hour event costs three time credits.

Between 2008 and 2009, members contributed 21,000 hours to running mother-and-toddler groups, after-school clubs, dance classes, a lantern festival, a pantomime, the creation of a public park and a sculpture, residential home visits and the community café. The earning and spending of time credits has transformed the popularity of the venue and united the community. In 2007, local people decided to reintroduce a local carnival. The last one had been in 1985, the year in which the last colliery was closed down. The theme was 'Our Valley's Heritage', a celebration of a proud community.

*'If we abandon the idea of community, we are destined to become shipwrecked on small social islands, modern-day Robinson Crusoes - increasingly isolated in DIY comfort zones of our own construction.'* **A. Osborne**, Local Writer and Member of the Blaengarw Timecentre

## Model three: agency-to-agency

Just like the special trading arrangements between suppliers and their wholesale customers in the business world, the 'agency-to-agency' model of Timebanking links organisations directly. They use time credits as a medium of exchange to share skills and resources, to collaborate, and share learning and assets with each other. This is a different type of mutual-credit system. Experiments are under way in the North of England, Wales and Gloucestershire. There has also been a great deal of interest in this model from social enterprises and networks of freelance workers. The Internet is used to inform organisations of the offers and requests, and to record the exchanges, which are valued in hours. Given the difficult times that are certainly ahead for voluntary organisations, using this model to swap skills and knowledge will be a great help in surviving the loss of grant aid that will come.

For a closer examination of models of Timebanking, visit **www.timebanking.org** and see Katharine Devitt's Masters dissertation on 'Sustainable Timebanking'.

## Our values

Joy and I knew that in order to create a sense of ownership and an identity for Timebanking it would be important to have a set of shared values to which people could sign up. So we adapted the core values of our mentors, Time-Banks USA, which are as follows:

**1 ALL PEOPLE ARE VALUABLE ASSETS:** Everyone can do something to improve the wellbeing of other people in their community. Don't therefore look for what people can't do or for what they need from you but, rather, find out what they are good at doing and help them find opportunities to share their skills, do well and feel useful.

**2 COMMUNITY BUILDING IS REAL WORK:** Bringing up children, keeping communities safe, caring for people and being an active citizen all need to be recognised as real work, to be shared, celebrated and rewarded.

**3 RECIPROCITY AND TRUST ARE OUR FOUNDATIONS:** Most people will repay a favour and will want to give something back to a community that offers them support. Wherever possible, 'you need me' must become 'we need each other'.

**4 SOCIAL CAPITAL GIVES US ACCESS TO OUR CULTURE:** Our social networks are the means by which we find out what is going on, where we fit in and who can help us. The more people we know, the more opportunities and new ideas will come our way. Side-by-side with others, we can build mutual understanding, friendship and security.

## Computers for the carbon community

Timebanking has made a major contribution to community life by using modern technology to re-invent the 'collective memory' that used to exist in every community. Many years ago, I lived in the mountains in Wales and everyone knew who was good for a favour (and who was not). Life happened all around us, and acts of hospitality and selfishness were remembered. We also had a shared information system about what skills different people had, and when and under what circumstances they were likely to be happy to share them. This is how things had been for generations – and not only in rural areas. Street maps of Victorian London had an index on the back of each page detailing who lived where and what skills and resources each household was willing to offer; for example, washing, repairs, cooking, clothes-making, wood-chopping, furniture-making, writing, baking and many others. Everyone could obtain most of everything they needed for cash, bartering or by exchanging favours without stepping out of the few streets around where they lived.

The 'Time Online' computer programme now acts both as a 'collective memory' and an 'information system' and can be used in any community.

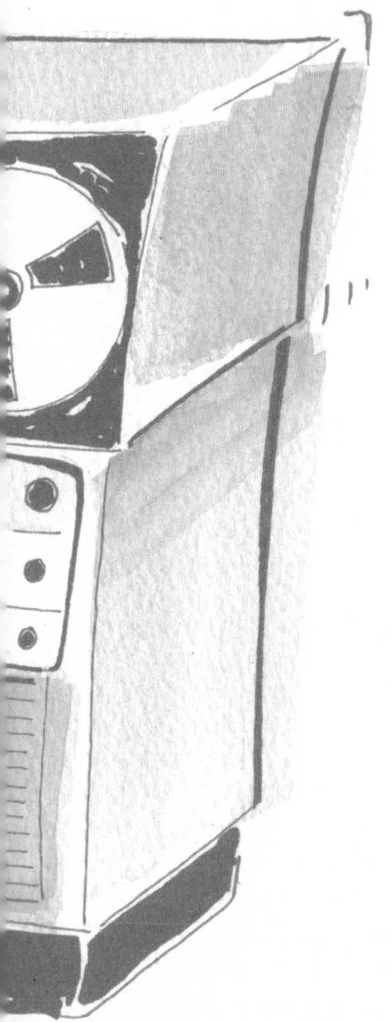

The first step, however, still requires human beings. Just as with community organising, the key to successful Timebanking is getting to know the people. At one-to-one interviews, or sometimes in groups, we invite local people to tell us what they would like to see happen in their community – what things they like doing and what skills they are interested in sharing; what are they likely to need help with in the future and what are they prepared to do for their community; how would they like to celebrate achievements? This and other practical information is stored on the computer so that in each area we know who is available, when, and with what skills.

From then on, whenever someone asks for a task to be done or to be put in contact with like-minded people (to take on a social issue, for example), the computer can immediately provide a list of members who are able, willing, interested and available to act. The Time Online system also connects all of the time banks around the country, so that at the press of a button people can see what skills are available both locally and nationally. There are plans to introduce many more features and applications, such as profiles of local people, comment walls, knowledge management and blogs for sharing wisdom. In the USA, New Zealand and the UK, people can also arrange to exchange services directly with each other online and see the profiles of other local members. In the UK we register everyone first in person, for safety purposes.

Text messaging is also being used to communicate with time-bank members to inform them of offers of help and requests from other members, and to contact others quickly when dealing with unforeseen emergencies.

A National Time Exchange is now up and running in the UK to transfer time credits across the country, wherever there is a time bank. People earn their time credits in their local neighbourhood and can send them to an elderly relative, for example, who may live in another part of the country and who can then use the same time credit to get an hour of the social care or practical support she or he needs from their local time bank.

People have also started international exchanges. UK citizens with relations in Australia and Africa are looking at how Timebanking can be used as a structure for self-help across the world. The time-based currency offers an equal basis for exchanging favours across frontiers and across national currencies, and the information system can connect people with each other across geographical and political boundaries. Their vision comprises a sharing and caring community across the world that exchanges skills and promotes trust, non-violence, respect and reciprocity.

## The human touch

In the description of Timebanking in practice, we have so far discussed the currency, a set of values, a computerised collective memory and an information system. What we need now is to look at the human qualities needed to be a good 'time-broker'.

Each and every time bank is shaped by the locality, by the people who join it and by the personality of the time-broker. Ideally a local person, (or a group of people), time-brokers are the keys to success. Time-brokers have to be motivators, facilitators and sometimes mediators. They do not need any academic qualifications, but they do need an ability to inspire others and to get on with people. They are people who can create a sense of adventure and instil in people the confidence to take a risk and get involved with something new. They help people to understand what the Timebanking values mean and they make sure that everyone both gives and receives in equal measure.

Time-brokers become the trusted intermediaries for people who find it hard to ask others for help. They need to be aware of how people are getting on, and whether assignments went well or not. They spend their time in building relationships and ensuring that there is a rich supply of stories to retell to attract newcomers and to nurture a sense of belonging for everyone. At a time bank everyone has a role to play. For an hour or two a month, not usually any more, each person helps to make things happen locally – things that everyone can point to with pride.

## What's in it for you?

Time-bank members report that they save time, save money, know more about what's going on locally, feel safer and less stressed, enjoy life more, get real satisfaction from sharing their skills, hobbies and interests, and really value the chances to try out new things and meet new people. The extent and range of activities that people share in a time bank are extraordinary.

One of the most valuable functions of a time bank is connecting the different generations. Only through older people sharing their stories with the younger generations will people develop a sense of local identity and keep their community alive.

Rita was 84 and finding it difficult to look after her large garden. To make things worse, her fence was constantly vandalised by the young people who hung around outside in the street. She felt unsafe and worried. Through her local time bank, she found some local people more than happy to give her a hand with the garden and to fix her fence. What's more, together they hatched a plan. Rather than view the local young people as a threat, they invited them in for a day to dig the garden. They offered them a free disposable camera each as a reward, and the adults and young people enjoyed a fun day together, culminating in a hilarious garden party. Word spread and young people now grow vegetables in the garden and look after it with Rita. Rita now feels very safe. The teenagers are now digging, sowing seeds, tending plants and distributing free food in the neighbourhood – all for the price of a few throwaway cameras and a hot meal cooked on a campfire.

I heard of a similar story from another time bank where generational boundaries were being broken down by a neat mutual exchange – older residents were teaching young people the skills needed to make themselves funky hats and scarves. In exchange, young people were teaching older people to send text messages!

The first city-wide time bank, Fair Shares Gloucester, hit the headlines during the floods when it was able to mobilise teams of 'volunteers'. The

*'We are all optimists and activists at a time bank.'*

**Dame Anita Roddick**, Founder of the Body Shop and Founding Patron of Timebanking UK

time bank teamed up with Radio Gloucestershire, which ran hourly bulletins and hundreds of people rang in requesting emergency help and offering to volunteer. Time-bank members can respond quickly and their local knowledge is invaluable in an emergency. Reyaz Limalia, the time-broker, organised the delivery of thousands of bottles of water that were essential; even in the middle of a flood, no-one had water to drink. In fact, time banks have been successfully used to mobilise people in Japan following earthquakes, and in Florida for hurricane relief.

Deborah's teenaged daughter was waiting for neurological surgery when their home in Gloucester was flooded. The council put them up in a B&B; however, as they now did not have a 'fit and proper home', the hospital told them that the operation would have to be postponed. Doctors, social workers and voluntary agencies offered their sympathy, but were powerless to help. Fortunately, Debbie and her daughter belonged to their local time bank and within days a rentable house was found, decorated and furnished by other local members. To everyone's relief, the operation could go ahead. Only through a time bank could they tap into the local knowledge, connections, energy, goodwill and skills that were required to respond swiftly and effectively to their emergency.

## Doing time

A local currency makes it possible for everyone to make a contribution, whatever their circumstances. At Gloucester Prison, inmates earn time credits refurbishing bicycles in the prison workshop, which are then sent to Iraq and given to people who need them. They make such a beautiful job of hand-painting the bikes that one of them was auctioned recently. The winning bid was for 100 time credits. Confined within a prison workshop, the inmates had generated 100 hours of care and support in their local community. That is a classic example of an 'ordinary miracle', achieved by the imaginative use of a

*'We have a team of residents in their seventies who like ironing and they are the backbone of the time bank. Another very popular service is mattress-turning.'* **Gloria**, Castlemilk Time Bank

complementary currency with a social purpose – it can travel through solid brick walls and connect up people with shared good intentions.

The inmates donate their time credits to a national goodwill pot or give them to their families to use. Fair Shares, the time bank involved, recommends that each prisoner keeps ten time credits for the time when they are released, to help them settle back into society. They have already earned the respect of a local social-support network at the time bank so their chances of staying out of trouble are wildly improved. This work in prisons is being rolled out across the country and has also been developed in Scotland by Gloria Murray and the Castlemilk Time Bank, which won the 'Queens Award for Volunteering' (the group equivalent of an MBE).

## Incentives and rewards for active citizens

The final elements of Timebanking are incentives and rewards for people making a contribution to their community. When we started, we were surprised to find that some people still insisted that we should not reward people for the good things they do. The volunteering culture has thankfully changed in recent years and now recognises that people respond well to praise and even better when they are given rewards.

Most time banks sign up local businesses, community organisations and councils. They can exchange resources through the time bank and offer incentives and rewards for the individual members. Tickets to sports events, theatres, cinemas, leisure centres, concerts and other places of interest are donated to the time bank; local businesses offer free services or reductions to say thank you for the effort time-bank members have put into making the area a safer, friendlier and more enjoyable place to work and live.

There are also other more emotional and long-lasting rewards that

*'The average happiness in one country compared with another can of people who say that other people can be trusted; the proportion the unemployment rate; the quality*

come from having people living nearby who care. For example, Michael has learning difficulties and a physical disability, which have often affected his confidence. He's been an active member of his local time bank and says that he has really enjoyed meeting new people. He has also earned time credits helping with events. When he was in the hospital for a few months, the time-bank members repainted two rooms in his flat so it was fresh and clean for him when he returned home. He now knows that he is a valued part of a local community that cares.

## The future

Timebanking is a new social framework in which everyone is viewed as an equal, and where the size of a bank balance buys no advantage. It takes place in a familiar 'social space' where good enough is OK. It presents opportunities to mix with new people in a friendly atmosphere. Those who want to can learn new practical, household, social, creative, political and survival skills. It is not only enjoyable and instructive to know what others are interested in and passionate about, but it is also life enhancing. As Diana Court, in New York, remarked over ten years ago: *'Sharing makes life itself a more joyful experience'*. Along with tens of thousands of other people, I have found that my local time bank has become a normal part of my weekly routine and keeps me in touch with a trusted, helpful, friendly, kind and respectful network of people who live in my area (and across the world). There is an old saying that goes something like this: when three people go for a walk, each one will return knowing something new; in Timebanking circles we say: When whole communities move forward together, the world will be transformed.

Time banks are incubators for a 'new compassion'. They breed a collective desire for change and infect the wider world with new possibilities.

*be largely explained by six key factors. These are: the proportion who belong to a social organisation; the divorce rate; of government; and religious belief.'* **Richard Layard**

The everyday acts of kindness, encouragement and skill-sharing generate further acts in a positive spiral that helps everyone to:

- feel connected and committed to the place where they live;
- share skills, save money and look out for neighbours;
- meet other people with a range of experience and knowledge;
- help each other to get well and stay healthy;
- build confidence and self-esteem;
- make life safer and more secure for everyone;
- deal with emergencies and get extra help;
- have happier lives and rewarding relationships;
- be more hospitable and have less fear of strangers;
- focus on the positive aspects of living in a strong community;
- feel good about themselves and be recognised as a kind person;
- ask for help when they need it and know they will have the chance to pay their community back; and
- protect the social environment for future generations.

With Timebanking, the bottom line is trust. We are social animals and, as such, we need and want to trust each other. Unfortunately, for many years levels of trust have fallen dramatically in this country. Richard Layard reports that in Britain today, the percentage of adults who think that most people can be trusted is half that of the 1950s.[53]

We know that Timebanking helps build trust and provides people with a vibrant local social organisation to which they can belong. We claim to be able to do little about divorce or unemployment rates, or religious beliefs. In time, however, we may persuade governments to trust people.

# Practical guidelines for successful Timebanking

There are now enough time banks around for you to take the first step on your journey, and go and visit one. Timebanking UK offers individuals and communities free nationwide training on setting up and running a time bank. Professionals are charged at a reasonable rate for this service.

The following list is loosely based on the guidelines by Philippe Granger at the Rushey Green Time Bank in South London:

## Making Your Time Bank Work[54]

1. Proclaim yourselves to be local 'social architects'.
2. Form a common vision of what your time bank will look like in five years.
3. Reach out across each other's social networks, the looser the better.
4. Visit other time banks and learn from them.
5. Start exchanging skills with each other from day one.
6. Involve people in recruiting other people.
7. Talk straight and avoid jargon. Be silent together whenever it is appropriate.
8. Refuse to believe people when they say they have nothing others would want.
9. Find out what everyone likes doing and what they need help with.
10. Remind people that it is important that they ask for services from others.
11. Remember onerous tasks are so much easier to do when they are shared.
12. Allocate tasks to people who are competent to do them and form task groups so people can learn new skills by working under the supervision of a more experienced and skilled person.
13. Time banks thrive on social events so have fun, eat together whenever you can and find something to celebrate every day.
14. The best ideas always come from the members so never stop listening to them.
15. Share out tasks as much as you can so that the time bank never becomes reliant on a few individuals.
16. When dealing with difficult people, it sometimes helps to keep in mind that they are likely to be thinking that you are the one who is being difficult.
17. Make it a collective responsibility to ensure the time bank runs smoothly and don't wait for people to be friendly; show them how.
18. Involve people in fundraising – they are your best advocates – it is their time bank and they will want it to continue.
19. Keep on sharing resources, building relationships and spreading information.
20. Collect stories about your adventures and retell them regularly.

## Carbon credits and time credits

Time-bank members have a growing reputation for green living. Environmental pollution is now attracting tax penalties and financial incentives are being offered to stop it happening. The social environment now requires similar large-scale resources to protect us all from social pollution. Investing in Time-banking is a good option, but maybe we need a better system than carbon credits as some companies and governments have already found ways of ducking their responsibilities. For a great parody of carbon credits visit **www.cheatneutral.com**, where you can offset marital infidelities against other people who are monogamous.

## Going green

Allotments, gardens and even window boxes are being used by time banks to grow food locally and any surplus is given away free. Other time banks plant trees, take on environmental clean-ups, undertake litter-picking, sort out waste, collect and help with recycling, and improve their local area by filling empty communal space with community gardens and hanging baskets. For example, Kirsty at the Caledonian Road Time Bank in London, organises massive street-litter pick-ups, for which participants earn time credits (and an energy-efficient light bulb each). At the North Cotswolds Time Bank, retired farmer Dave teaches local play-school children to grow food.

The Dinas Time Bank in South Wales adopted a riverbank and a train station. Michelle at the Lancaster Time Bank organised a meeting at the train station where Brief Encounters was filmed to prompt the recollections of their older members. The stories of their war experiences encouraged some army cadets to join; they now litter-pick around the football stadium after matches in exchange for group transport (and free tickets to a Victorian butterfly sanctuary). Jon at the Avalon Time Bank in Glastonbury is very skilled and extremely successful in actively promoting all aspects of green living.

In Rotterdam and in Curitiba (Brazil), people are paid in time credits for recycling and litter-picking; the tokens they receive in return can be used for paying for rides on buses so that spare capacity in the transport system is being used to motivate a clean-up of the city streets. Smart.

*'Timebanking helped us to stitch together lots of initially different and separate examples of activism - challenging planning applications, trying to create allotments, a grow-your-own-food project, and land-share and gardening in communal spaces.'* **Alan**, Yorkshire

## Two wolves

One evening an old Cherokee told his grandson about a battle that goes on inside people.

He said, *'My son, the battle is between two wolves inside us all. One is Evil: it is envy, jealousy, sorrow, regret, greed, arrogance, self-pity, guilt, resentment, inferiority, lies, false pride, superiority, and ego. The other is Good: it is joy, peace, love, hope, serenity, humility, kindness, benevolence, empathy, generosity, truth, compassion and faith.'*

The grandson thought about it for a minute and then asked his grandfather, *'Which wolf wins?'*

The old Cherokee simply replied, *'The one you feed.'*

# Chapter 6
# A global movement: stories from other countries

*'What we love, others will love*
*And we will show them how.'* **William Wordsworth**

**IN 1996, I went to the first-ever Timebanking congress in the USA, which was held in Portland, Maine. When the organisers heard that Masako Kubota, who heads up the Timebanking movement in Japan, was there – and that I was there from Britain – they declared it to be an international event. Timebanking has since spread to 22 countries and this chapter can only offer a glimpse of the variety of ways that it is being used around the world – and of its potential to be a global social innovation.**

## USA

The first time bank I ever visited was in New York. It was in a middle-class area near Fifth Avenue, and was run by a large voluntary organisation called Caring Community. The members of the time bank were mainly older people who lived on their own in apartments. The organisers trained members in simple active listening skills. The newly-trained 'barefoot counsellors' earned their time credits by visiting and listening to dozens of residents, one-by-one, who might otherwise have been isolated or depressed. They shared a culture and similar life stories and everyone valued the visits highly. As one resident told me, *'We understand each other and she has plenty of time for me; I love her.'*

More recently in New York, the local newspapers describe the time-bank groups set up by the Visiting Nurse Service as 'mini-United Nations gatherings', where exchanges are continually bridging traditional divides of nationality, language, ethnicity, gender, age and class. Mashi Blech, who is one of the original pioneers of Timebanking, is the driving force behind this groundbreaking work.

In Washington DC, the Time Dollar Youth Court handles over 65 percent of non-violent juvenile crime. First-time offenders are given the choice of attending the Youth Court to be tried by their peers. They then earn time dollars for sitting as jurors themselves and can use the time credits to pay for a variety of learning and recreational activities; for example, attending summer camps. Recidivism has gone down by more than 50 percent and the young people respond positively to being trusted and given a responsible role. As one former offender, serving as a juror, told an official from the Juvenile Justice Board: *'I learned my acts had consequences.'*

In 2009, I visited the Dane County Time Bank in Wisconsin and met Stephanie Rearick, the tireless organiser of over 500 members. I learned how Timebanking was creating opportunities for local people to use their creativity and compassion to solve social problems. Members of the time bank earn time dollars for running meditation and non-violent communication workshops in two prisons. In return, prison inmates have been working with Dane County Humane Society and are paid in time dollars to train stray dogs.

## A Timebanking anthem

In Timebanking features in learned journals, Mashi is often credited with a profound statement that has entered into our folk law: 'Often you can't buy what you really need. You can't hire a new best friend. You can't buy somebody you can talk to over the phone when you are worried about surgery.'

Mashi claims she never made this comment, but it has become something of an anthem for Timebanking in general. What she did say was this: 'I am also just launching a time bank in my neighbourhood – Ground Zero, Manhattan. This neighbourhood has clearly been significantly affected by a world tragedy. It is a relatively young neighbourhood, developed from scratch within the past 20 years. While most of the people are professional and middle to upper class, it has been hard hit by the recession and many people are now out of work or worried that they will lose their jobs. The time bank is perceived by community leaders to be a tool that could link the various neighbourhood groups (e.g., parents, seniors and young professionals).'

'We have all met many people we wouldn't have come in contact
We now need more ways for a larger percentage of the population
locations, Internet kiosks, mobile phone access and debit cards

## Taiwan

In Taiwan, the new emphasis on volunteer service as a system of mutual help has found expression in the concept of time banks. The goal of volunteer work has been expanded from helping underprivileged individuals to providing solutions for social issues. People are now motivated to improve communities and society as a whole, and more individuals choose community service (from recycling at a local community level to national initiatives to slow global warming) than any other form of volunteering. People are paid with Mutual Help Coupons with face values of 10, 30 and 60 minutes, which they then use to purchase services from others. Everyone gives and receives services. Lin Yi-ying, the Executive Director, says that the interaction and warmth created through the exchange of services builds strong communities. Senior citizens in particular benefit through receiving services – and also by giving them.

Lin Yuan-yuan calls the senior citizens that he and his wife Lai-chuan look after 'Old Buddhas'. He says he has learned a great deal of wisdom from them and the experience has taught him to be a better person.

*'Being continuously reminded of the value of their lives through the exchange of services, seniors come to understand their lives are actually more meaningful than they think,'* said Lin.

The Mutual Help Coupons must be spent in the same year in which they are earned, either by purchasing services or donated items at the foundation's year-end flea market. The senior citizens have come up with many new ideas for services – leading early-morning exercises in the community, making quilts and performing 'soul restorations', which are traditional rituals aimed at bolstering the psyche of those who have received a shock, or encountered other disturbing situations. The time bank also offers early-morning wake-up calls to students at Hungkuang University. Debbie Huang, Secretary General of the International Association for Volunteer Effort, says that working together to improve society in this way has changed her life.

*'I've become more active and positive. I've learned that when individual dreams become collective goals, nothing is too difficult to accomplish,'* she said.

*with and have formed strong bonds and a new level of compassion. to interface with the time bank, including drop-in street-level (dual-currency debit cards that record the time dollars people earn which entitle them to discounts at local shops).'* **Stephanie**, Dane County

## Senegal

In 1995, Pape Samb set up a group in Kaolack to create employment opportunities for women in a very conservative Muslim neighbourhood. GRADES (Group of Reflection and Action for the Development of Senegal) provides training to improve skills, unite communities and empower women and girls to help themselves. Women have few other opportunities. Through GRADES, women 'participate in essential decision-making processes and their needs are equally taken into account in designing programmes for the community'. GRADES runs a Timebanking programme and women use time credits to purchase services (use of a computer lab and sewing centre, and day-care for children) one hour at a time. They earn the time credits in a variety of ways and attend training sessions in literacy, nutrition and an interest-free loan scheme; they also learn how to transform native vegetation into jams and syrups to sell.

This is the only economic system to which the women have access, and it has proved very valuable to them. Women are gaining influence and more control over their lives and men are now open to communicating with the women 'about issues that impact on both sexes'.

Muslim leaders have 'embraced and endorsed GRADES and the time bank'. They have seen 'the positive economic impact that empowering women has had in their communities, without sacrificing tradition or religious beliefs'.

GRADES now operates in seven regions of Senegal and has 13 'chapters'. In just one they have created 48 jobs and trained 1,600 women. It is supported by the Phelps Stokes Foundation[55], which believes that 'education depends on respect for human dignity, the development of each human being, and the cultivation of social harmony'.

*'Perhaps the only limits to the human mind are those we believe in.'* **Willis W. Harman**

## Japan

The Nippon Active Life Club (NALC) has been Timebanking for 15 years and has 26,000 members at 130 local bases all over Japan. Such large numbers allow members to exchange time credits across the country so that family members in other cities may use them. At first there were fears that Timebanking would ruin the goodwill of volunteerism, but this has not proved to be the case. In 2001, for example, NALC members served 118,000 hours of traditional volunteering, while claiming 90,000 hours in the Timebanking system. By 2005, traditional hours had reached 192,000, while Timebanking hours climbed to 160,000. NALC interpret the statistics as showing that it is through the time bank that 'people have found the sheer happiness of helping others'.

There are over 300 Timebanking/LETS schemes in Japan. Space is at a premium in the cities and older people often have to leave and resettle in the country when they retire. Their children, who are still living in the cities, can earn time credits by helping in their local urban neighbourhoods. The government social services make sure that each time credit earned is honoured by an hour's social-care service where their older relations live in the rural areas. If the time bank cannot provide the service, a government agency does; in effect, it is underwriting the social currency.

On the smaller islands, people have their own version of Timebanking. Everyone receives 30 beautifully painted tokens at the beginning of the year and when they have received a service from another person they ceremoniously hand them a token: 'a ticket for a caring relationship'. At the end of each year, everyone gathers together for a celebration and a count-up of each person's tokens – they then redistribute them, giving everyone their 30 tokens for the coming year.

# Argentina

The Community Hours Bank in Capilla del Monte, Argentina, is the brainchild of Marcelo Mario Caldano, one of the most delightful people I have ever met. The town is in a remote mountainous area and, here, 40 families came together as they needed a kindergarten and a primary school for their children. 20 percent of the funds required came from the community itself. Another 40 percent came from the parents contributing time to a co-operative that was a partner in the scheme. (The parents contributed, for example, by packaging and distributing local organic honey.) The final 40 percent came from the Community Hours Bank.

The families took on all of the activities at the school that they could not afford to pay for – such as administration, repairs and maintenance, childcare and extra teaching in weaving, carpentry, painting and folk dancing. They then created a system for paying for the costs of these jobs through the Community Hours Bank. A new currency called 'Soles' was used and parents were paid partly in cash and partly in Soles for undertaking the tasks needed at the school. They can use Soles to buy services from each other, exchange them at fortnightly fairs and pay for items from the co-operative. The commitment of the parents has been so reliable that the co-operative now issues cash grants to needy community members that are guaranteed by the value of the in-kind donations from the community members.

*'Basically one wants to feel that ones life has amounted to more than just consuming products and generating garbage.'* **Henry Spira**

# Israel

Timebanking started in Israel in 2002, and there are now 42 time banks, with new ones opening at the rate of six each year. In Jerusalem, there are 12 time banks and Gideon, the main organiser, has been delighted to have recently opened a time bank in a very orthodox Haredi (community), as well as a time bank in a local Arab community. Women have been the driving force behind these initiatives. For many people, life has become harder very quickly in recent years, and the gap between the rich and poor has widened. The breakthrough came with the realisation that the tradition in Judaism of giving to the poor and one-way volunteerism was not good enough anymore. In Timebanking they found a system that nurtured solidarity and actually solved social problems by using reciprocity to develop community ties and strong communities.

It's worth noting, too, that in the UK, Jewish Care celebrated its 150th anniversary in 2009. The largest Jewish health and social care charity in the UK, and 66th largest charity in the country as a whole, it provides services every week to 7,000 people. In a recent speech delivered in Israel, Neil Taylor, the Chief Executive, said, *'Timebanking provides an excellent opportunity to fulfil our two main goals; to engage people and to reach out to marginalised and isolated communities.'*

Taylor continued, *'Timebanking, which we hope to develop within the context of our community centres, is a model of work without walls.'*

*'We are bigger than our schedules.'* **Paulo Freire**

## Spain

Timebanking in Spain has grown out of the women's movement and is now well established. Rather than offer a snapshot of their activities, I will end this chapter with a challenge from the Spanish Timebanking movement. This has been abridged from a paper distributed at a Timebanking conference in Barcelona, by the Universidad Internacional de Andalucia:[56]

## Are our times to be driven by the market or by the rhythms of nature?

Our conception of time is changing. There has been a shift from cyclical time set by the rhythms of nature to a mechanistic time driven by clocks. Add in changes in our sense of space, brought about by high-speed transport, a new urbanism and instant communication systems, and we realise that distances have been reduced and time has been compressed. Human beings are part of nature and their wellbeing depends on nature's flow of services. The failure to take into account nature's limits has led to the collapse of some civilisations that came before us.

Uncontrolled growth has led to an imbalance between nature and society.

There are now two competing cultures of time: the instantaneous accelerated culture and the culture of respecting nature's time, including our own nature as living beings. Daily caring, relationships and community life take place in cyclical time and sustain the future. But these activities are now considered secondary. Cyclical time is shared and versatile and the real value of time invested in caring is in the process itself.

However, in the modern world, time is viewed as a scarce possession for individual and exclusive use. But, time expands when it is shared. A good example of this is the Timebanking experience, where skills and services are

freely exchanged and value is measured in hours, not by money or the type of activity. Yet each day we continue dedicating the best quality time of our lives to paid work, not to personal and social development. Consumerism forces us to work more. Years go by, and we are never masters of our own time. Even children are losing their free time. Their time must now be planned and they are seldom left to play, to have their own adventures, make discoveries and take risks.

Can we live once again as though time mattered to us? It is a question of values, but also of resistance and opposition to unsustainable ways of life. Our responsibility is both individual and collective: by changing our way of managing our time we decide on priorities and apply values. Our choices can influence the marketplace and political decision-making. The personal is political. We need to see our decision to live by a new culture of time as positive, something that will enrich us. What we might lose in material goods, we will gain in time. It is not a backward step to look after the family and social relations that we are losing because of our hurry. We can live better with less; give time as a gift, dedicate time to play, to the arts, to food, to friendship, to nature, to ourselves, to others.

# Chapter 7
# How we do it in time

*'The future is like everything else, it isn't what it used to be.'* **Charles Kettering**

**AS THE PACE OF CHANGE in the world accelerates, it is crucial to strengthen the social environment if we are to have the resilience to cope with and shape the changes, rather than being shaped by change we don't actually want. Safe, healthy and creative societies require people to engage actively as citizens. For this to happen, local, neutral and public spaces are needed, along with a fairer and modern system for pooling skills, experience, knowledge and ideas.**

By repopulating a communal life, people will be better able to achieve a comfortable balance between their considerable abilities to compete in the marketplace, and their more natural inclinations to co-operate.

## Getting to young people

In future, we hope that Timebanking will be taken up by more schools.

There are a few that already run time banks and there is enormous scope for future development. Young people need to experience first-hand the benefits of mutuality, to experience a more balanced lifestyle – part consumer and part citizen.

In North London, Hargrave Park Primary School ran a time bank for several years. In the playground, there was a designated buddy bench where troubled pupils could sit. Older pupils were trained in active listening and in simple conflict-resolution techniques. They also acted as playground storytellers. For providing all these services to the younger pupils, they were paid time credits. They also trained parents how to use computers. In return, the parents ran sports-coaching, gardening and bike maintenance sessions, for which the school and the pupils paid in time credits. Time credits were also used to pay for end-of-term treats, like horse-riding.

In Brixton, young people are earning time credits cultivating window boxes and any unused space they can find to grow food. There is plenty of scope to expand these urban mini-allotments, they calculate that there are 35 acres yet to make use of in London alone. Simon, who runs the EcoStars time bank, remembers the early days of the project when three of the young people were getting ready to go with him to another part of Lewisham to buy garden supplies.

The young people each automatically picked a hammer out of the toolbox to take with them. They were, after all, going into another postcode! Simon has worked hard, and these three young people are now key members of the group and a constant inspiration to others. The EcoStars has grown, moved on and shared many community experiences using Timebanking. The present team have just designed and planted the winter garden outside the Festival Hall. Their logo is proudly on display in the centre of London outside a major cultural venue, alongside the logo of a very proud Timebanking UK.

The Timebanking network now stretches across the country and when some young people in a time bank in Cornwall heard about what the EcoStars were doing in London, they invited them down for surfing lessons as a reward. What goes around comes around.

We urgently need to find other ways to bring the increasing number of 'displaced and misplaced children' in the 'global village' back in touch with their local communities. Otherwise, it is very likely that the break-up of our social environment will soon inflict a great deal of social pain on everyone.

In her 1970s novel, The Four-Gated City, Doris Lessing vividly describes a London where adults no longer venture out onto the streets for fear of young people. There are 'feral' children living on the streets of the capital right now, and Saturday nights in city centres are already no-go areas.

Will there have to be some absolutely catastrophic events to shock people into action before a social climate change can take place on any significant scale? There is common agreement that things are going seriously wrong and, with Timebanking, we have a credible way forward. We all need, therefore, to acknowledge that we are at a 'tipping point' in our social history. Society is in danger of moving towards an 'ice age' that will threaten the survival of our capacity for mutuality. We need mass action to create a great 'social warming', before we all drown in our indifference toward the wellbeing of others.

*'Species that survive and prosper are ultimately those that find a niche in which they meet their own needs in ways that simultaneously serve others.'* **Margulis** and **Sagan**[57]

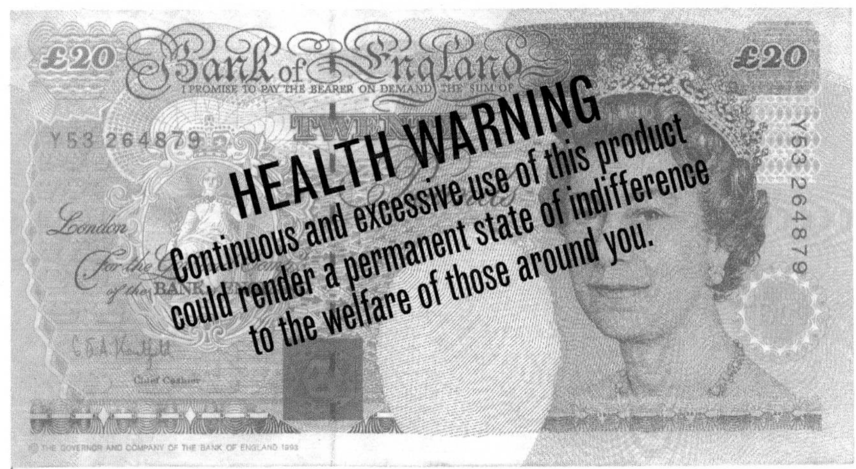


## Timebanking for a social warming

The Timebanking movement developed as a response to the growing gulf between public services, the public and those whom the services aim to help. Politicians and professionals are failing to harness the potential within communities for mutual support, by not recognising or trusting in people's abilities. A damaging consequence has been an undermining of people's trust in themselves, and each other.

Yet, according to David Boyle and Andrew Simms, in their book The New Economics[58], the world is developing the 'seeds of a new economics', visible in 'downshifting' and a demand for ethical, local and sustainable food, business and trade. This is all restoring respect for the interconnectedness of people, locally and globally.

*'We face social and ecological imperatives distinctive to this moment in the human experience to embrace the higher potentials of our nature … our understanding of the interdependent nature of our relationships to one another and the planet.'* **David Korten**[59]

## Time for each other

Timebanking (the currency, the values, the social networks, the software, the incentives and the time-brokers) is a revolutionary process that is transforming neighbourhoods. There are now over 200 time banks across the UK; each one is a unique response to the various abilities, aspirations and requirements of the locality. Already over 20,000 people have joined a local time bank.

In future, there will be many different models, drawing on the creativity and skills of local people in local communities and people from various interest groups. What they will all have in common is a set of shared values and an economic system based on equality and justice. Whatever the skills and abilities involved one hour's action equals one time credit: one = one.

*'Where is the wisdom we have lost in knowledge? Where is the knowledge we have lost in information?'*

**T. S. Eliot**[60]

## A place for modern technology

Timebanking has the potential to help people to expand their understanding of the place where they live, and their connections with the people who live there. It is about more than exchanging skills; Timebanking is about changing lives. It is about turning strangers into friends and friends into social activists.

The Internet has revolutionised the way we spend our time, what we know, who we know and how we conduct our relationships. In a short story called 'The Time Machine', written over 50 years ago, E. M. Forster predicted a society where we all lived in individual capsules underground. Technology provided us with food and took care of all of our physical needs, and we communicated with each other through computer screens. The trouble was that we lost touch with our humanity. People had no sense of any responsibility for each other, and had few obligations to family and friends – and no form of interaction with the natural world.

William Gibson, the writer who first coined the phrase 'cyberspace',

described it as a 'consensual hallucination' – a place where people could suspend their disbelief and fantasise that they were together with friends having normal relationships in 'communities'. Is the consensual hallucination becoming a bit too real?

Are we seriously going to leave the fate of our social environment to government, the marketplace and technology? My guess is that the best they will come up with is CCTV cameras in our houses, a must-have interactive 'robot buddy' for each of us, and implants in our brains that set off an alarm at a call centre when we drop dead.

As discussed earlier, Timebanking software holds a new version of the collective memory that people shared when they lived in stable communities that encouraged sharing, mutual trust and common regard. In the future, every community can host a flexible, comprehensive and speedy communication network – a local time bank to facilitate the exchange of skills and favours, as well as news, opinions and ideas. Through electronic forums, mobile phones and digital television, local people can reconnect with each other through their time bank, and learn about the place where they live – and the people next door.

In the past, the rapid advances in technology were exploited by computer experts who were often more comfortable with machines than people, and products were marketed as replacements for genuine relationships. The aim of Timebanking is to use technological advances to reach beyond information-gathering and entertainment, and connect people emotionally to the places where they live, and to nurture the needs of the user for face-to-face contact with others.

We now have these new ways to communicate with each other – 'social media' – and if it is used well it can proliferate our sharing and empower us to take collective action without the need to go though formal organisations and traditional institutions. This is truly revolutionary. I have been so impressed, for example, by how in Bristol recently, a young man sent out a message to his Facebook friends and beyond, announcing that on the next Sunday he would be going to some local woods where fly-tipping had become a serious problem, and pointing out that he intended to start to reclaim the area by clearing it up. A thousand people turned up to help him.

In the introduction to this book, I described how Barack Obama used the Internet to turn three million well-wishers into active advocates. (My favourite story was of him asking his young supporters to go home at the weekend and persuade their grandparents to vote for him.) In this country, campaigners are slowly switching on to the organising power of the Internet. Hope not Hate, the anti-BNP group, which operates with a small team of four full-time staff, recently used the social media to organise volunteers to distribute over three million leaflets by hand.

The digital divide is narrowing and emails and mobile phones are now familiar and convenient tools available to a great many people. What we still need to appreciate is their capacity to overcome many of the current obstacles to identifying and contacting each other, and co-ordinating collective action, as and when it is needed.

Timebanking has embraced these communication tools and is using them to co-ordinate more caring and sharing in communities, and to reclaim public spaces for citizens to express themselves, enjoy each other's company and break away from an unhealthy dependency on money.

In his book, Here Comes Everybody[61], Clay Shirky expands on our shared vision: '*We don't often talk about love when trying to describe the public world, because love seems too squishy and too private. What has happened, though, and what is still happening in our historical moment, is that love has become a lot less squishy and a lot less private … We can affect the people we love, but the longevity and social distance of love are both constrained. Or were constrained – now we can do things for strangers who do things for us, at a low enough cost to make that kind of behaviour attractive, and those effects can last well beyond our original contribution. Our social tools (i.e., Internet, mobile phones and websites) are turning love into a renewable building material. When people care enough, they can come together and accomplish things of a scope and longevity that were previously impossible; they can do big things for love.*'

# Bridging the two economies

Many companies have donated goods and services to time banks as rewards for the hours people have spent community-building. The benefits have been mutual. For time banks, it has meant an additional way of saying thank you to participants and provided even more incentive for new people to get involved.

For the companies, it has provided a means by which they can enhance their reputation for social responsibility, motivate their staff and increase customer loyalty. In-house Timebanking within companies could improve staff relations and job satisfaction levels even more, and become a rewarding way for employees to widen their experience and deepen their contact with local community. Timebanking can also be used to orchestrate the exchange of resources and skills between companies.

Our high streets, shops, coffee bars and offices could play a vital new role in protecting our social environment and provide space for people to meet and explore new ways to share skills, ideas, knowledge and experiences. In Real England, Paul Kingsnorth described the customers in his grandparents' shop: *'They talked, they gossiped. They shared stories, exchanged tips, offered and received help, extended invitations, did all the things people do when they get together as equals … This is what makes local shops, cafés, pubs and other such gathering places the arbiters of place and community. Talk to any independent shop-owner and they will tell you that they do a lot more than sell things to people … [it's about] being flexible, approachable, part of the community. Being human.'*

The entrances to supermarkets, for example, could host Timebanking Internet kiosks, with information attractively displayed on electronic screens to bring alive the wealth of contacts, exchanges and inspirational activities available in the local area – and to celebrate the hours of care and practical support that have been exchanged each week by local people. Volunteering, caring and citizenship would be brought in out of the cold and back into the marketplace. Corporate social responsibility could become more than short-term, episodic acts of charitable giving. It could help to transform society and be a key player in saving the social environment for future generations. Neighbourhood forums and parish councils could contribute financially to expand their networks out into community; a single penny on local council tax could fund a time bank in every street in every town, in villages and in city centres.

When businesses and communities work together, new ideas will be certain to emerge. Maybe the 'Big Society' concept by the Coalition Government will provide the springboard. One new idea we are working on right now is an 'application' for mobile phones so that customers could show a retailer the time credits they have earned and receive a discount on goods and services in recognition of their contribution to the local community.

## Spreading the word about a great social warming

Timebanking has spread by word of mouth and is now slowly being taken out into the public arena. Advertising and marketing have been particularly effective at maintaining brand loyalty for companies and it is time for this expertise to be employed to generate a desire for a new loyalty to each other and to our neighbourhoods. Positive messages about trust, mutuality and respect need to be articulated throughout society, by word of mouth and by the media.

Everyone has a part to play in this emerging new order, and small groups of people can change history. Those in power dismiss social movements as a threat to the status quo, as unthinking, dangerous and unpredictable. Yet a mass acceptance of the need to restore some sense of mutuality in society and an appreciation of our common citizenship is the only way we have any chance of saving the social environment.

We used to live in social environments that were shaped by people, the physical place, the climate, the natural resources and the culture. Each place was unique and the people living there identified with it and felt some responsibility towards its upkeep. But now we all live in a 'global nowhere' and we are all in danger of forgetting our roots. We are not building any sort of future together with the people who live around us and the longer we don't the harder it is to imagine why we should. We have lost our way in the street where we live and distract ourselves looking for today's bargain in the high street. Even more foolishly, we continue to place our faith in a corporate machine that is geared up to maximise profits and minimise risks to come up with all the answers. Just like in our favourite children's stories, we suspend our disbelief and convince ourselves that whatever happens and however terrible life is at the moment, we will all live 'happily ever after'. We hope that those in power will ultimately act responsibly, exercise self-restraint and be straight with us if and when things are getting completely out of hand. Unfortunately, we are as deluded as they are - just like children in a sweet factory, they cannot and will not stop stuffing their pockets.

As Ghandi said: *'A certain degree of physical comfort is necessary, but above a certain level it becomes a hindrance instead of a help; therefore, the ideal of creating an unlimited number of wants and satisfying them seems to be a delusion and a trap. The satisfaction of one's physical needs must come at a certain point to a dead stop, before it degenerates into physical decadence. Europeans will have to remodel their outlook if they are not to perish under the weight of the comforts to which they are becoming slaves.'*[62]

Over-indulged children have serious attachment problems in later life because their families never asked them to make a contribution. They did not share in any household chores or take on any responsibility for others; they never received praise for being a valued and integral part of the family group. As a result, they did not feel connected or that they belonged.

Timebanking is helping people to find a new way back to co-sufficiency, to make a contribution and to be valued. People are becoming reconnected and developing a local identity for themselves and for the area where they live. As a friend said to me recently: *'If you want to see a lot, standing in one spot is a good way to do it.'*

# Borrowing from the future

The acts of 'give and take' that Timebanking is built around remind all involved that blaming others is pointless and that if we want to 'live happily ever after' we have to spend time and effort every day improving the nature and extent of our relationships with others. Timebanking is giving expression to the value we place in our common future. It is a step in the right direction – towards each other. As Philip Larkin so eloquently wrote: 'virtue is social'.

A persistent 'I-cocooner' may insist that there just isn't enough time to be a neighbour or active citizen. Actually, there is an increasing amount of time available. For example, the legal European working week is becoming shorter.

And I hope this book has shown you how you can share time, save time, spend time, give it away or even recycle it:

*'By Timebanking it would become possible to neutralise that vexing characteristic of time, that it "runs away". Meaning it cannot be saved up. With timebanking it is possible to transfer time to the future – to originate a claim on the future work of others by investing one's own time now, a claim that could be cashed in later when one's own time was at even more of a premium.'* Offe and Heinze [63]

Of one thing you can be sure; when you are on your deathbed you are not going to be wishing you had spent more time worrying or watching TV. You may regret, however, that you did not respond positively to the challenge laid down by our Spanish friends and summarised in Chapter 6: *'Are our times to be driven by the market or by the rhythms of nature?'*

Offe and Heinze published their classic book in 1992 and it was the first time I had seen the proposition that just as capitalism has colonised the developing world it is setting about colonising our 'core economy' of family, friends, colleagues, neighbours and community.

The 'free market' has become the dominant supply system to each of our separate households and money is the primary means of exchange of articles of everyday use. We no longer exchange things directly between households, or, if we do, somehow they are seen as second best and the exchange regarded as a short-term emergency solution. We have allowed the free market to decide for us what is produced, what is consumed and what price we should pay for it. This has limited our individual freedoms and weakened our natural inclination to be generous.

In The Value of Nothing, Raj Patel quotes a recent study:
***'In many North American indigenous cultures, generosity is a central behaviour in a broader social and economic system. One anecdotal account examined what happened when boys from white and Lakota communities received a pair of lollipops each. Both sets of boys put the first one straight into their mouths. The white boys put the second one in their pockets, while the Native American boys presented it to the nearest boy who didn't have one. It's not surprising to see that culture can shape how resources are accumulated and distributed, and dictate the social priority of saving over sharing, but the experiment also reminds us that the opposite of consumption isn't thrift – it's generosity.'***[64]

It saddens me to report that we have found that some people in this country do not believe that they have anything worthwhile to offer others. There is also a widespread feeling of powerlessness and a common felt belief that this carefully evolved democracy of ours leaves little space for Her Majesty's subjects to play any useful or meaningful part. As Edgar Cahn has said: ***'Reasonable solutions would be easy if there were a consensus that national governments could be trusted to reward rather than exploit volunteerism.'***

## Power With not Power Over

I believe that we have to stop viewing power as a negative force. Power is simply the ability to act, no more, no less and in itself is completely neutral. Frances Moore Lappe, a community organiser and Timebanking enthusiast, asks us to rethink power.[65]

### RETHINKING POWER

| POWER IS | POWER CAN BE |
|---|---|
| Zero sum. It strengthens some people at the expense of others. It divides what already exists | Mutually expanding. It builds the capacities of all involved. It is creative, generating new strengths and new possibilties |
| A one-way force: either you have it, or you don't. Life boils down to the powerful versus the powerless | A give and take, two-way relationship. No-one is ever completely powerless because each person's actions affect others |
| Limiting, intimidating and scary | Freeing |
| Controlling | Collaborative |
| Rigid, static | Dynamic, always changing |
| Derived mostly from laws, status, force and wealth | Derived from relationships, knowledge, experience, numbers, organisation, creativity, vision, perseverance, discipline, humour and more |
| About what I can do or get right now | Mindful of creating and sustaining relational power over time |

Ed Chambers, the community organising leading light, urges us to come to terms with the fact that there will always be a tension between the world as it is and the world as we believe it should be; a gap between our values and the reality of everyday life. Therefore we must learn to 'live well' with this tension and refuse to be 'condemned either to materialism or false idealism'.[66]

He illustrates this point by looking at the two key drivers of social action often mistakenly viewed as opposites: *'Power and love – like self-interest and self-sacrifice – are not mutually exclusive... There can be no creative power without some acknowledgement of the other's interests, just as there can be no healthy love if the self is wholly lost in concern for the other. Reinhold Niebuhr had it right. "Power without love is tyranny and love without power is sentimentality." In power and love, the interests of both parties matter. Understanding the relational character of power and love transforms the practice of both because both require give and take relationships. Power and love are two-way streets.'* Ed Chambers

## Changing our cultural story

In 2007 Thomas Greco visited Bali and found that community life there was still vibrant and their social networks were extremely resilient.[67] The villages and townships looked after themselves, without much interference from the central government or the need for extensive public services. Others have reported that the people in Bali are happier than people on nearby islands. Why is this so? How have they resisted the lure of the 'here and now consumption' that has overtaken so many neighbouring islands? The answer is, in great part, because everyone belongs to a 'Banjar' – a local circle of co-operation – just as they have all done for centuries. They use time as a currency. Everyone gives a few hours freely each week and everyone has access to all the resources they need. The bonds between families and communities are constantly renewed.

In the Banjar everyone is regarded as an equal and everyone feels a part of something bigger than themselves. Timebanking is our modern equivalent of a Banjar so there will never be a truly broken Britain because we know how to fix it. All we need to do is change our cultural story.

*'In all the social movements I have studied across the world, every one appreciates the importance of maintaining, curating, developing and celebrating not only the physical resources but their culture, understanding both the material and the cultural worlds as bodies on whose shoulders everyone stands, and which everyone is free to use, share and build upon.'* RAJ PATEL [68]

A few years ago Richard Rockefeller, a supporter of Timebanking in the USA, sent me a copy of an 18th century English folk poem:

*'They hang the man and flog the woman*
*That steal the goose from off the common,*
*But let the greater villain loose*
*That steals the common from the goose.'*

I thought of this poem after laughing out loud at the Woody Allen remark quoted in Raj Patel's book: 'I am at two with nature'. The next day I was flicking through another book, one on working with groups by Keith Tudor,[69] and read: *'Next fall, when you see geese heading south for the winter, flying along in "V" formation, you might consider what science has discovered as to why they fly that way. As each bird flaps its wings, it creates an uplift for the bird immediately following. By flying in a "V" formation, the whole flock adds at least 70% greater flying range than if each bird flew on its own. If we have as much sense as a goose, we will stay in formation with those people who are headed the same way we are. When the head goose gets tired, it rotates back in the wing and another goose flies at point. It is sensible to take turns doing demanding jobs, whether with people or with geese flying south.'*

I leave the final word to our Founding Patron:

*'We need a time bank in every town and to do that we need to proselytise. I want routes to solutions and this community here today is one of the most profound routes to solutions I have ever come across.'*

**Dame Anita Roddick,**
speaking at a
Timebanking Conference[70]

# Endnotes

**1** Jonathan Rowe is a writer living in Washington DC. His article in The Ecologist, from which this quote was taken, was called 'Prozac or Park Benches'. See www.ecolgist.org. His article in the New Internationalist (November, 2000), called 'Eat, Sleep, Buy, Die' was also influential.

**2** Emmy Werner is Professor Emeritus at the Department of Human and Community Development at the University of California at Davis. She lead a 40-year study of 698 infants on the Hawaiian island of Kauai and found that one-third of all high-risk children displayed resilience and developed into caring, competent and confident adults. She identified protective factors in the lives of these resilient individuals, such as a strong bond with a non-parent caretaker (such as an aunt, babysitter or teacher) and involvement in a church or community group, which helped to balance out risk factors at critical periods in their development. Her quote is taken from The Power of Resilience, by Brooks and Goldstein (Contemporary Books, 2004).

**3** Janisse Ray's article, 'Local Economics: The source of true security might be closer than we think' appeared in Hope Magazine in May 2003 (www.hopemag.com). Janisse was the first to coin the word 'co-sufficiency' and, in her article, simply states the profound insight that money gives us a kind of power and freedom, but so does friendship!

**4** John McKnight's quote comes from the opening remarks he made at a conference in Nova Scotia, Canada, in July 2009, entitled 'Community Capacities and Community Necessities'. He is Co-Director of the Asset-Based Community Development Institute in the USA. I also recommend his article 'John Deere and the Bereavement Counselor', published in 1984 by the E. F. Schumacher Society. Visit www.smallisbeautiful.org/publications.html.

**5** The Earth Charter is an international declaration of fundamental values and principles considered useful by its supporters for building a just, sustainable, and peaceful global society in the 21st century. Visit www.earthcharterinaction.org.

**6** In his classic bestseller, When Corporations Rule the World, David Korten exposed the destructive and oppressive nature of the global corporate economy. In his later book, The Great Turning (Kumarian Press and BK, 2006), from which this quote comes, he argues that the organisation of society through hierarchy and violence is not the natural order of things and we can turn away from it.

**7** Paul Kingsnorth is an environmentalist and author of Real England: The Battle Against the Bland (Portobello Books, 2008). Visit www.realengland.co.uk.

**8** A study in Chicago, by the Harvard School of Public Health (published in the August 1997 issue of Science), concluded that by far the largest predictor of the violent crime rate was 'collective efficacy' – a willingness by residents to intervene in the lives of children and more specifically, a willingness to stop acts like truancy, graffiti painting and street-corner 'hanging' by teenage gangs. The study examined 343 neighbourhoods in Chicago and interviewed 8,872 residents. One of the study's authors noted that 'collective efficacy' stems from a 'shared vision, if you will, a fusion of shared willingness of residents to intervene and social trust, a sense of engagement and ownership of public space'. The critical factor in terms of violence was not 'external actions', such as a police crackdown, but the 'effectiveness of "informal" mechanisms by which residents themselves achieve public order'. See 'The Co-production Imperative', a report by David Boyle at the Timebanking UK website: www.timebanking.org.

**9** The Spirit Level: Why more equal societies do better, by Richard Wilkinson and Kate Pickett (Penguin, 2009).

**10** Q.v. note 4.

**11** The Future of Money: Creating a new wealth, work and a wiser world, by Bernard Lietaer (Century, 2001).

**12** Edgar Cahn, as quoted in 'Money: Print your own', published in YES!: A journal of positive futures, Spring edition, 1997.

**13** Revolutionary Wealth; How it will be created and how it will change our lives, by Alvin and Heidi Toffler (Alfred A. Knopf, 2006). They coined the word 'prosumers' to describe people who consume what they themselves produce.

**14** Money, Heart and Mind: Financial wellbeing for people and planet, by William Bloom (Viking, 1995).

**15** Beyond Employment, Time, Work and the Informal Economy, by Offe and Heinze (Temple University Press, 1992).

**16** Q.v. note 20.

**17** 'I Cocoon' was originally used by many writers as a clever play on words but I now find that 'I Cocoons' are on the way for real, or do I mean for virtual? A major software company is currently developing the 'Immersive Cocoon', a human-sized pod akin to those seen in The Fly series of movies. Although CNN has discussed the 'I Cocoon' being the next generation of computer interfaces, the 'I Cocoon' is actually designed with video games in mind, literally. Its immersion and interactivity definitely represent what's in store, at least conceptually. Will they fit neatly side by side on the Tube or at the farmers' market, I wonder?

**18** All Consuming: How shopping got us into this mess and how we can find our way out, by Neal Lawson (Penguin, 2009). According to research by the recruitment website Gumtree, we spend £18 billion a year on domestic care. One in three Britons pays someone else to work in their home, whether gardening, cleaning, housekeeping or childcare. Half of all parents employ domestic help. We are outsourcing the running of our families.

**19** Deep Economy: Economics as if the world mattered, by Bill McKibben (One World, 2007).

**20** Money Matters: Putting the eco into economics – global crisis and local solutions, by David Boyle (Sawday; Fragile Earth, 2009)

**21** Q.v. note 7.

**22** Q.v. note 19.

**23** Alison Hawthorne Deming, published in Getting to Maybe: How the world is changed, by Westley, Zimmerman and Patton (Vintage Canada, 2007).

**24** On Kindness, by Adam Phillips and Barbara Taylor (Hamish Hamilton, 2009). As the philosopher Alan Ryan writes, 'We mutually belong to one another', and the good life is one 'that reflects this truth'.

**25** Happiness: Lessons from a new science, by Richard Layard (Penguin, 2005).

**26** 'Somebody's Baby', a short story in the collection entitled High Tide in Tucson: Essays from now or never, by Barbara Kingsolver (Harper Collins, 1995). 'We are blazing a bold downhill path from the high ground of "human collective", toward a tight little den of "self".'

**27** Mothers and Others: The evolutionary origins of mutual understanding, by Sarah Blaffer Hrdy, (Harvard University Press, 2009).

**28** 'The Selfless Gene', by Olivia Hudson, published in The Best American Science and Nature Writing (Houghton Mifflin, 2008).

**29** The quote from Maggie Jackson was in the media, as she promoted her new book written with Bill McKibben, entitled, Distracted: The erosion of attention and the coming dark age (Prometheus, 2009).

**30** Visit www.demos.co.uk.

**31** Q.v. note 7.

**32** American Mania, by Peter Whybrow (W. W. Norton & Co., 2005).

**33** YOU ARE Therefore I AM: A Declaration of Dependence, by Satish Kumar (Green Books, 2008). 'From you I receive, to you I give. Together we share, by this we live.'

**34** Beyond Globalisation: Shaping a sustainable global economy, by Hazel Henderson (Kumarian Press, 1999).

**35** The Crisis of Global Capitalism, by George Soros (Little Brown & Co., 1998).

**36** 'Fundraising from the Heart', by Lynne Twist (The Soul of Money Institute, 2004); visit www.soulofmoney.org.

**37** Edgar Cahn, keynote speech at the Association of Directors of Adult Social Services and Local Government Association Conference: 'Communities that Care, Services that Deliver', Newcastle. Visit www.timebanking.org.

**38** Q.v. note 13.

**39** Q.v. note 4.

**40** Neither Victims or Executioners, by Albert Camus (New Society, 1986). His book The Plague was responsible for many people (including myself) realising that if we wanted to change the world it was up to us.

**41** David Boyle, as quoted in The Time Of Our Lives: Using Timebanking for neighbourhood renewal and community capacity building, by Gill Seyfang and Karen Smith (New Economics Foundation, 2002).

**42** Bowling Alone, The Collapse and Revival of American Community, by Robert D. Putnam (Simon & Schuster, 2000).

**43** 'The New Wealth of Time: How Timebanking helps people build better public services', by Josh Ryan-Collins, Lucie Stephens and Anna Coote (New Economics Foundation, 2008).

**44** 'State of Loneliness: The government's new public services reforms focus on rights and entitlements, but supportive relationships are key to tackling social ills', by Charles Leadbeater (The Guardian, 1 July 2009).

**45** No More Throwaway People: The co-production imperative, by Edgar S. Cahn (Essential Books, 2000).

**46** In 2008, the New Economics Foundation was commissioned by the Foresight Project on Mental Capital and Wellbeing to review the work of 400 scientists from across the world in order to identify a set of evidence-based actions that will improve wellbeing. The findings are available as attractive postcards written by Jody Aked, Nic Marks and Corrina Cordon.

**47** Q.v. note 25.

**48** Happy Planet Index is a study of human wellbeing in 178 countries, which was published by the New Economics Foundation in 2006. Visit www.happyplanetindex.org.

**49** Time Dollars, by Edgar Cahn and Jonathan Rowe (Rodale, 1992).

**50** Spiritual Currency: Building a new economy with volunteer credits, by Derek Brownlee (Northlink, 1993).

**51** Funny Money: In search of alternative cash, by David Boyle (Harper Collins, 1999).

**52** Community Currency Guide, by Bernard Lietaer and Gwendolyn Hallsmith (Global Community Initiatives, 2006). Visit www.global-community.org.

**53** Q.v. note 25.

**54** 'Making Your Time Bank Work', by Philippe Granger (Rushey Green Time Bank, 2009); winners of the London Health Commission Award and the Sustainable City Award.

**55** Phelps Stokes Foundation; visit www.phelpsstokes.org/.

**56** Abridged from an article by Ramon Antunez, Maria Jose Bautista-Cerro, Edith Checa, Isabel Gonzalez Turmo, Elvira Mendez, Carlos Montes, Maria Nova, Mauro Pizzato and Frencesco Tonucci; visit www.unia.es/content/view/800/542/.

**57** Microcosmos: Four billion years of evolution from our microbial ancestors, by Lynn Margulis and Dorian Sagan (Summit Books, 1986).

**58** The New Economics, by David Boyle and Andrew Simms (Earthscan, 2009).

**59** Q.v. note 6.

**60** The Rock, by T. S. Eliot (Faber & Faber, 1934).

**61** Here Comes Everybody: How change happens when people come together, by Clay Shirky (Penguin, 2008).

**62** Q.v. note 33.

**63** Q.v. note 15.

**64** The Value of Nothing, How to reshape market society and redefine democracy, by Raj Patel (Portobello Books, 2009).

**65** Getting A Grip, clarity creativity and courage in a world gone mad, by Frances Moore Lappe (Small Planet Media Books, 2007).

**66** Roots for Radicals, Organising for Power, Action and Justice, by Edward T. Chambers (Continuum Publishing, 2008).

**67** The End of Money, And the future of civilisation, by Thomas H. Greco Jr (Chelsea Green Publishing, 2009).

**68** Q.v. note 64.

**69** Group Counselling, by Keith Tudor, (Sage Publications, 1999).
*"The red-breasted goose has suffered a staggering 56% population decline in the last 10 years. It is at high risk of extinction in the wild."* Wildfowl and Wetlands Trust, Slimbridge, Gloucestershire

**70** 'It's About Time', Conference Report Time Banking UK, Birmingham, 2001. See www.anitaroddick.com - the land of the free.